SACRIFICIAL LOVE
His Will Our Inheritance

By Lynn E. Sheldon

TITLE: SACRIFICIAL LOVE

Author: Lynn E. Sheldon

Published by: GodFire Revival and Discipleship Outreach

Published in (USA)

ISBN: 978-0-578-22763-4

All verses are from the **English Standard Version (ESV),** unless otherwise noted.

The Holy Bible, English Standard Version. ESV® Text Edition: 2016. Copyright © 2001 by Crossway Bibles, a publishing ministry of Good News Publishers.

KJV (Public Domain)

PREFACE

"It always seems inexplicable to me that those who claim free will so very boldly for man should not also allow some free will to God. Why should not Jesus Christ have the right to choose his own bride?"

Charles Spurgeon

ACKNOWLEDGMENTS

I wrote this book in remembrance of my brother, Lonnie, who was younger by birth but older in the faith. He taught me the true meaning of salvation and how it takes place. Afterward, he challenged me to seek the truth.

Lonnie shared God's plan of salvation with me over the phone. And I admit his three-hour phone calls to teach me parts of His plan eventually put me to sleep. Sensing I had fallen asleep on him, I can still hear him say, "Lynn, you did not go to sleep on me, did you? It was the most important part. I will need to go over it again." Embarrassed, I would reply, "But Lonnie, it has been three hours. Sorry, it's great stuff, but I dozed off near the end."

So, after three years, Lonnie's view began to make sense, so I spent time studying the Word to see if his teaching had any merit. And to my surprise, God's Word confirmed my brother's view about salvation.

Now, after fourteen years studying this subject, I would like to share with you what I discovered through the guidance of the Holy Spirit, and Lonnie's perseverance. His teaching placed me on the path to seek the truth about God's plan to save a people for Himself through Christ.

So, I dedicate this book to my brother, who is now with the Lord, and my Heavenly Father, who entrusted me to write this book for you and for Jesus Christ, who suffered in our place so that we might have eternal life.

Thank you for your interest in this book. I pray it will open your eyes to God's plan to save us and give us hope beyond the grave.

TABLE OF CONTENTS

INTRODUCTION

"Do your best to present yourself to God as one approved, a worker who does not need to be ashamed, rightly handling the word of truth."

2 TIMOTHY 2:15

As Christians, we must follow God's Word by adequately interpreting it. Unfortunately, this does not appear to be happening today. Instead, many believers purposely misinterpret the Word to justify their beliefs or behaviors. In doing so, they create a god-like idol in their minds. Is this a new phenomenon? No, it's not. According to Solomon, "There is nothing new under the sun (Eccl. 1:9). And Psalm 50:21 says, "These things you have done, and I have been silent; you thought that I was one like yourself. But now I rebuke you and lay the charge before you."

BUILDING ON THE RIGHT FOUNDATION

Being a teacher, I never share a new truth with others unless I have done my research to make sure what I have heard or read has been interpreted correctly. Yet, many believers do not take this approach.

Instead, they pass along what they hear or see without any concern about accuracy, or they twist God's Word to justify their thinking or behavior.

With little thought about context, they misuse God's Word to support their beliefs or activities. By misleading their flock, they send them down a path our God never intended them to follow.

Spreading questionable doctrine is nothing new. These doctrinal differences, over the last 2,000 years, have created various church denominations that reflect their founders' approach to God's Word. Paul addressed these variances formed around men and not God.

In First Corinthians 1:11-15, Paul writes, "For it has been reported to me by Chloe's people that there is quarreling among you, my brothers. What I mean is that each one of you says, 'I follow Paul,' or 'I follow Apollos,' or 'I follow Cephas,' or 'I follow Christ.' Is Christ divided? Was Paul crucified for you? Or were you baptized in the name of Paul? I thank God that I baptized none of you except Crispus and Gaius, so that no one may say that you were baptized in my name."

The Apostle noticed how water baptism divided believers, where they began to follow different teachers. Such divisions, like the one Paul referenced, formed the various Christian denominations we have today.

For instance, regarding baptisms, some denominations say sprinkling suffices, while others say we need to immerse believers in water. Still, others believe baptism is necessary for salvation, while some think it's symbolic of our death, burial, and resurrection in Christ.

Other disagreements include such doctrine as the security of the believer, spiritual gifts, water baptism, and the salvation process, to name a few.

Unfortunately, most Christians blindly identify with their founders without searching for the truth. And while these denominations use God's Word to defend their beliefs, as in the case of water baptism, they cannot all be aligned with God's Word.

Therefore, instead of accepting a denomination's position without thinking it through, it's our responsibility to find the truth. Meaning, we need to seek the truth and receive it, even if it differs from our church founder's or someone else's beliefs.

THE REASON I WROTE THIS BOOK

I spent the last 14 years studying God's salvation plan, writing articles, and participating in discussions involving His plan. Over a year ago, the Lord led me to write this book to help you see God's plan of salvation from His perspective, rather than someone else's.

For instance, when I speak about salvation, people ask me if I follow Arminius or Calvin. I tell them, "Neither! I'm a follower of Christ." And as for God's plan of salvation, the Word presents the facts, so I decided to spend time searching for answers to God's plan of salvation and related views such as the rapture, the Millennial Kingdom, and the new heaven and a new earth. After reading this, you might consider doing the same.

WHAT YOU WILL DISCOVER IN THIS BOOK

I shared how this book is the culmination of a 14-year study, so you can imagine how excited I am to share with you what God has taught me over the years. Do I have a monopoly on these truths? No! To make such a claim would sound arrogant on my part. My purpose for writing this book is to simplify God's perspective regarding His plan, from Genesis to Revelation, and to convey how consistent His plan is throughout the Word.

SOME SHOCKING TRUTHS

What I discovered may shock some of you. If it does, you are not alone. My brother introduced me to some of these truths, and it took him three years to convince me to consider them, do my research, and eventually write about what I learned.

Thus, I invite you to please read the entire book to see the truths unfold in the same manner God gave them to me. When you do, you will discover how God's plan is His. And because it is, He remains active in pursuing it and bringing it to fruition just as He envisioned.

The Lord commands us to love one another and to seek the lost. We are to share the gospel so they might receive God's gift of salvation. Yet, we must remember, we are not God. As believers, we are, but the vessels He chooses to share the good news with others. Salvation is God's plan; therefore, we must be careful to impart it according to His Word.

If you have questions about what you are reading, you will probably find the answers as the truths unfold throughout this book. Plus, you will not want to miss a new perspective on God's salvation plan, which He gave me to share with you in Chapter 10. It's a game-changer!

WHY THESE TRUTHS ARE IMPORTANT

Thank you for taking the time to read this book. We need to understand God's plan of salvation correctly because of the entirety of His Word centers around it. Being central to the entire Word of God, many of the doctrinal differences we have stems from the way we view God's plan of salvation. These differences will remain until we see it from His perspective.

As you read this book, I pray God opens your eyes to His plan, just as He did for me. I could not have written this without prayer and the hunger I had to discover the truth. It's my hope this book will offer you a path to follow, so you, too, may seek the truth about His saving grace and the plan He gave us, in Christ.

Section I
THE PLAN

"...declaring the end from the beginning and from ancient times things not yet done, saying, 'My counsel shall stand, and I will accomplish all my purpose,'"

ISAIAH 46:10

1

THE BEGINNING

"I will put enmity between you and the woman, and between your offspring and her offspring; he shall bruise your head, and you shall bruise his heel."

GENESIS 3:15

From the beginning, God had a plan to redeem humanity from its fallen state by providing a Savior who will come between the woman's offspring (children) and the serpent's offspring (the wicked). This Savior bruises the head of the snake by crushing his empire and triumphing over sin and death.

MY STRUGGLE WITH ADAM AND EVE'S FAILURE

The story of Adam and Eve is a mystery to most of us. For instance, I never understood why Adam and Eve had to fail. I, like many of you, assumed God created them to live forever?

Having struggled to find an answer, I knew there had to be a higher purpose for Adam and Eve's rebellious behavior, but I could not figure it out. While I realized they had to fail to usher in Christ, I wanted to know why He did not allow them to forego the forbidden fruit and, instead, let them eat from the tree of life and live forever in their innocent state.

In my quest to find the truth, I kept coming up empty-handed, so I turned to the Lord and said, "Lord, why did Adam and Eve have to die?" The Lord remained silent until one morning, after finishing my prayer and Bible study, He spoke and said, "Lynn, if you want to understand Genesis, you must apply James 1:13-14." In other words, He wanted me to apply James to Adam and Eve's plight.

Wondering what these verses had to do with Adam and Eve's downfall, I turned to them and read, "Let no one say when he is tempted, 'I am being tempted by God, for God cannot be tempted with evil, and he himself tempts no one. But each person is tempted when he is lured and enticed by his own desire'" (James 1:13-14).

After reading these verses and meditating on them, I understood why God wanted me to connect them to the Genesis story. In doing so, my view regarding Adam and Eve's failure and God's eternal plan changed for the better; and I pray this book will do the same for you.

2

NO COINCIDENCE

"Let no one say when he is tempted, "I am being tempted by God," for God cannot be tempted with evil, and he himself tempts no one."

JAMES 1:13

Nothing about God's economy is an accident or a coincidence; this includes placing Adam, Eve, and Satan on the same planet. Why did God do this? We find the answer in James 1:13. It says God cannot tempt us with sin. And since He cannot do this, He placed Satan, Adam, and Eve on the same planet, so Satan could tempt Adam and Eve to test their hearts and fulfill His plan of salvation for humankind.

As for Satan and his demons, their weapon of choice is temptation. By diligently doing their homework, they stalk us and learn what we like and dislike while watching us and listening to our conversations and self-talk. And because of their research, Satan and his demons never have to guess what bait to use. Instead, they gather what they have learned and use this information to develop their plan.

GOD NEEDED ADAM AND EVE TO FAIL

Applying James 1:13-14 to Genesis, I discovered why God needed Adam and Eve to fail. To make sure it happened, God gave Adam a "Don't" command and created the necessary desire to set up Adam and Eve for their ruin.

As for Satan's part, he brought God's plan to fruition when he tempted Eve. Knowing this, the Bible says, "But each person is tempted when he is lured and enticed by his own desire" (James 1:14).

James 1:14 says when we lust for something, Satan will tempt us where we desire. And this yearning to have what God forbids leaves us open to demonic temptations. The fallout can be more than what we bargained for when we take the bait and sin. Likewise, as you will see, Adam and Eve thought Satan held the answer to their need. But it was all a lie, and they suffered greatly for entertaining his deceptive offer, and so do we when we look to the world for answers and not God.

ADAM UNDERSTOOD GOD

Before the fall, Adam and God had a mutual relationship. God told Adam what he needed to do, and Adam did it. In other words, Adam had no problem understanding God's commands because the human spirit, like a radio tuned to the right frequency, made it easy for Adam to communicate with God. However, Adam and Eve's ability to hear God ended after they sinned. Yes, sin caused their human spirit to become blind to the things of God. And as far as we know, God never again spoke to them directly or indirectly after He drove them from the garden (Gen. 3:24).

God Puts His Plan of Salvation in Motion

The plan of salvation began when God exiled Satan from heaven to a formless and void planet called Earth, as punishment for his rebellion against the Lord. Isaiah 14:12 says, "How you have fallen from heaven, morning star, son of the dawn! You have been cast down to earth, you who once laid low the nations!" And while we do not know how many years Satan occupied this planet before God created Adam, we can assume it was long enough to make Satan think this planet was his kingdom, and he is the one who reigns over it. But all this was about to change.

CREATING PARADISE

When Satan saw this formless and void planet turn into a magnificent paradise, I can only imagine how thrilling it was for him to see this happen. But, as the story unfolds, the exuberance Satan felt on the fifth day must have evaporated on the sixth when God created Adam and gave him authority over Satan's self-proclaimed planet must have blind-sided the Devil.

Giving Adam authority over this planet had to anger Satan. Why? Because having failed to take over heaven, he was not about to lose his domain to this newcomer, and this is something he was not going to put up with from him. So, the old serpent began to develop a strategy to dethrone Adam and return this paradise to its rightful owner, himself.

GOD GIVES AUTHORITY TO ADAM

"And God said, 'Behold, I have given you every plant yielding seed that is on the face of all the earth, and every tree with seed in its fruit. You shall have them for food.'" GENESIS 1:29

Before casting him out of the garden, God gave Adam authority over His creation, including seed yielding plants, and those with them in their fruits. Because they were not meat eaters, trees provided them the food source necessary to sustain life.

GOD SETS THE TRAP

In Genesis Chapter 2, God placed Adam in the garden and ordered a mist to flow over it. As the plants grew, He asked Adam to tend the garden; and for the moment, everything looked positive for God's new creation.

But one day, "God commanded the man saying, 'You may surely eat of every tree of the garden, but of the tree of the knowledge of good and evil you shall not eat, for in the day that you eat of it you shall surely die.'" (Gen. 2:16-17)

God gave Adam a command, unlike any he had previously given him. What made this one different? Until now, His orders were "Do" instructions, which were easy for Adam to carry out. But this directive was different because it established God's authority over Adam and removed Adam's control over this one tree. And as you will see, Adam did not take this loss lightly.

A "DON'T" COMMAND SPARKS REBELLION WITHIN

Most people believe God created Adam and Eve to live forever, and the two blew it. Is this what happened? Well, instead of having them live forever, God orchestrated their failure to fulfill His plan and purpose.

The Bible says, "The power of sin is the law" (1 Cor. 15:56). What does this mean? Put yourself in Adam's place for a moment. Think back to a time when your parents told you not to do something, and afterward, all you could do was think about the command they gave you and how to break it without them finding out. Or, think about God's Ten Commandments. How many times have you broken them over your lifetime? If you are like me, it would be too numerous to count.

Now, if you know how difficult it is to keep God's commands, can you imagine the resentment Adam must have felt when God told him not to eat from that tree? Consequently, the forbidden fruit became Adam's, and later Eve's obsession because God's creation lacks the willpower to keep this command. And because it ignites the power of sin within, God used it to set His eternal plan in motion.

GOD CREATES EVE

"Then the Lord God said, 'It is not good that the man should be alone; I will make him a helper fit for him.'"
GENESIS 2:18

After giving Adam the order, God asked him to name the creatures He had formed from the ground. Knowing this would keep Adam occupied, God also decided to give him a helpmate after Adam asked Him why he was the only creature who did not have one. So, God created woman from Adam's rib, and Adam called her Eve (Gen. 2:18-23).

I chuckled at the timing of Eve's appearance. Why? By waiting to give Adam a helpmate after the 'Don't' command, I could not help but think how God used her beauty to take the edge off Adam's concern over the loss of this one tree, at least for the time being.

3

THE FALL

"Now the serpent was more crafty than any other beast of the field that the LORD God had made."

GENESIS 3:1

God set up Adam and Eve to fail by giving Him a Don't command. This mandate must have set up Adam to the point where He complained about it to Eve. You may ask, "How can this be? The Bible says nothing about Adam's reaction to the command." You are right; it does not. But to understand God's plan, here is where we insert James 1:13-14.

I mentioned how Satan tempts us where we desire. And he never wastes his time tempting us with something we do not covet or lust after because we would ignore his temptations. Also, I shared how Satan and his demons do their research by listening to us speak and observing our actions while they stalk us to determine the perfect bait to entice us with so we will fall to their evil scheme.

Once they know what they need to do, Satan and his demons choose the perfect bait to seduce us to act on our desires. By doing this, Satan and his demons can render us powerless, in our strength, to resist their targeted temptations, and so we bite.

How Temptation Works

Let me illustrate how important it is for Satan to make the right offer when tempting someone. I spent 47 years in radio sales. And over the years, I wrote thousands of ads for clients. Some ads worked, and some did not.

So, what differentiated a successful ad from an unsuccessful one? A successful advertisement attracts attention by offering the right message, at the right time, for the right price. If our listeners needed the product, they would listen to the ad and respond. If not, they tuned it out.

As you can see, Satan's temptations and radio ads have the same goal in mind. Both succeed when a person has a need or desire for the product advertised or, in this case, Satan's offer. To regain his kingdom, Satan knew he would need to make an offer Eve could not refuse.

Applying James to Genesis

By applying James 1:13-14 to Genesis, and knowing how temptation works, it had to trouble Adam to lose his authority over this tree. But you say, "Lynn, it was just one tree." I know, but it reminds me of the time I misplaced a twenty-dollar bill. I looked everywhere for it. Although I could have driven to the bank to withdraw another twenty, I did not. Instead, I needed to find the one I misplaced. So, I never stopped looking for it until I did. Why? Because what mattered to me was the loss and not the amount.

Wondering if Adam may have felt the same way, I revisited Genesis, Chapter 3. Knowing Satan always uses the right bait, I decided Adam must have said to Eve, "If I were like God, I would not have lost this tree." Hearing him complain about it had to stoke Eve's curiosity. So, in Genesis Chapter 3, we find her standing next to the tree, primed to discover what made it so special.

Eve Scouts Out the Tree

"Did God actually say, 'You shall not eat of any tree in the garden?'" On cue, she responds by saying, "We may eat of the fruit of the trees in the garden but God said, 'You shall not eat of the fruit of the tree that is in the midst of the garden, neither shall you touch it, lest you die.'" GENESIS 3:1-3

In Chapter 3, Satan hides near the tree, waiting for Eve to arrive. How did he know she would be there? By stalking Adam and Eve, I imagine Satan either noticed how she reacted to Adam's warning about the tree, or this serpent knew she would visit the tree because of something she said. Anyway, wherever he got the information he needed to put together his strategy to take her down, the only thing left was for her to show up.

Finally, she arrives. While staring at the tree, an unknown voice catches her attention by twisting God's Word to get her to react. Observations from this encounter, in Genesis 3:1-3, offer us some important clues: First, Satan knew God told Adam not to eat from the tree in the middle of the garden. Again, the Devil either heard God give Adam this command, or he overheard Adam warning Eve about the forbidden fruit.

Next, Satan's plan to stir Eve to talk included misstating God's Word to gain a reaction from her. When she heard him misspeak, she corrected him and then distorted God's command by adding to it; for God never mentioned anything about touching the fruit. As for her misquote, you will see how it worked to Satan's advantage in setting Eve up to fail.

After gaining her confidence, the old serpent convinced Eve she would not die (Gen 3:4). He then offered her the right bait and set the hook with these words, "You will surely not die. For God knows that when you eat of it your eyes will be opened, and you will be like God, knowing good and evil" (Gen. 3:4-5).

Feeding into her curiosity, Satan made it sound a[...] had withheld something from them. Plus, the old serpent [...] have struck gold with the words, "...be like God."

With all the fuss over this tree, Eve knew there had to be [...] something unique about it and its fruit. After all, it looked good, and it was a delight to the eyes. Plus, according to Satan, if she ate from this tree, *she could be like God.* So, without hesitating, Eve picked the fruit, ate it, and she did not die. No doubt, Satan was pleased. He had made his case, gave her the right bait, and now he was on his way to regain his planet. Yep, one down, and one to go.

SCARCITY IGNITES OUR LUST-FILLED DESIRES

While I gave up beer 34 years ago, I recall a time during my college years when my fraternity brothers heard about a new brand hitting the market in our area. They could not wait to try it. But there was a problem; until the state approved the sale of it in Missouri, it remained illegal to buy the brand locally.

Because we attended a college located in Missouri, my fraternity brothers could not buy it locally. So, to satisfy their curiosity, they planned a ninety-minute trip to Kansas City, Kansas, where they could finally drink the forbidden brand and enjoy it legally.

When we arrived at a popular Kansas City pub, my brothers ordered the brand. By the smiles on their faces, I could tell this brand was worth the trip. However, being the designated driver, I had no idea what made it so special, but apparently, they did.

After a few hours, the adventure came to an end. It was late, so we loaded up and headed back to our fraternity house. While on our way, my brothers used the ninety-minute drive to plan their next trip to Kansas, where they would once again enjoy what they called, "the best brand ever."

t trip never happened because what my
d for occurred. Missouri finally approved
nd, enabling them to purchase it locally.
they could not wait to buy it.

I now know what made the brand so
...as not the formula, but the scarcity and a
"Don't" command, given by the state, made it *the best brand ever*.

If you think about it, my brothers had the same reaction Eve had toward the forbidden fruit. In both cases, a "Don't" command made both the brand, and the fruit from the forbidden tree, unique. Yet, after Missouri approved the sale of this beer, the brand's distinct appeal faded away. Once it became just another brand, my brothers lost their interest in it, and they returned to their former brands.

EVE'S HAUNTING MISQUOTE

I mentioned how Eve's misquote worked against her. You might be wondering how. Well, it's not complicated. To pick the fruit, she first had to touch it. And when she did, nothing happened to her.

Surviving the touch must have given Eve the green light to take a bite from the forbidden fruit, and again, nothing happened to her. No doubt, she came to the point where she believed Satan and ignored God's command. I am guessing we have all been there.

Yes, when we fall to Satan's temptations, we experience a moment of insanity. And like Eve, we ignore God and side with our tempters until our guilt and shame overcome us, then we regain our senses, repent, and seek God's forgiveness. So, it's not difficult for us to relate to Eve's plight; and how she so quickly gave in to Satan's temptation. While she did it once, I have no idea how many times I have given into temptation.

ADAM OBSERVED THE ENTIRE ORDEAL

The temptation scene, in Genesis Chapter 3, makes us think Eve was there by herself. Until she tempted him, we had no idea Adam was standing behind her.

Knowing he was there, I found it interesting how he never cautioned her or tried to stop her from eating the fruit by knocking it from her hand. Instead, he remained subdued until she turned and tempted him to take a bite.

Like a coward, Adam stayed behind his "damsel in distress," as he anxiously waited for her to take the first bite. And why not let her do this? After all, if she survived the ordeal, then he could eat from the tree. If not, well, she broke the command, not him. His inaction proves Adam wanted what Satan had to offer. He observed the ordeal, heard the serpent tempt Eve by telling her she could be like God, and did nothing to restrain her.

Seeing Eve survive the trial must have encouraged him to take a bite. And without any hesitation on his part, Adam took the fruit from Eve and ate it. Why? He believed Satan had the answer to his need to be like God and regain his authority over the tree. But, as we know, this bite did not turn out the way he thought it would.

THE BITE CHANGED EVERYTHING

When Adam bit, everything changed. As far as we know, this tree's fruit was no different from the other fruit in the garden. So, what triggered the change? It took his disobedience to activate their consciences, where they came to know right from wrong just as Satan predicted.

Once their rebellious actions stirred their consciences, both Adam and Eve knew they were naked, and they felt ashamed. Fearing what might happen to them, they covered themselves with leaves and hid from God (Gen. 3:10).

Instead of Adam reclaiming his authority, God called them out of their hiding place, brought charges against them, cursed them, removed their leaves, dressed them in animal skins, and banished both Adam and Eve from the garden forever. Yes, Adam's rebellion cost them everything, including their lives. Eventually, they died just as God said they would (Gen. 3:12-24).

ADAM, THE FEDERAL HEAD

Why did Eve's rebellious act not affect her right away? It did not because Adam received the direct order from God, not Eve. The Lord warned Adam by saying, "For in the day that *you* eat of it, you shall surely die" (Gen. 2:17). Therefore, until Adam ate from the tree, nothing happened to them. But after he took a bite, their rebellious act ignited their consciences, and they felt ashamed.

Because of Adam's position as the federal head over Eve and every person since then, except Christ, he had the responsibility to make sure both he and Eve carried out God's command. But when he failed to do this, it tainted them and their entire offspring with a death sentence no one can escape.

THE TREE OF LIFE

"Now, lest he reach out his hand and take also of the tree of life and eat and live forever—therefore the Lord God sent him out from the garden of Eden to work the ground from which he was taken. He drove out the man, and at the east of the garden of Eden he placed the cherubim and a flaming sword that turned every way to guard the way to the tree of life." GENESIS 3:22-24

After His creation fell, God made sure Adam and Eve would never, again, have access to the tree of life. To accomplish this, God drove them out of the garden forever. And to prevent them from returning and eating from this tree, God ordered His cherubim and a flaming sword to guard it.

Now, had they eaten from the tree of life, after they sinned, both Adam and Eve, and their entire offspring would have lived forever in their sinful state, making it impossible for God to redeem them because they could not die. As you will see, without the ability to suffer death, the only destiny for humanity would have been the lake of fire.

A WHAT-IF FANTASY

One day, I asked God the following question: "What if you had never given Adam and Eve a 'Don't' command but allowed them to eat from the tree of life and live forever, what then?"

God answered this question by asking me if angels can sin. I told Him they can, for the Bible tells us when Lucifer (Satan) tried to seat himself above God, the Father kicked him, and the angels who followed him, out of heaven (Isa. 14:12, Rev. 12:7-14). And since angels cannot die, making them unredeemable, the Lord will one day toss Lucifer and the fallen angels into the lake of fire where they will remain forever.

Having the ability to live forever would not have kept Adam and Eve from sinning. God told me if He had given Adam a "Don't" command, after eating from the tree of life, Satan would have tempted them, and they would have fallen, making all humanity unredeemable because, like the angels, they could not die.

Meaning it did not matter whether Adam and Eve had eaten from the tree of life and then sinned, or they ate from this tree after they sinned; both options would have tainted humanity, making redemption an impossibility. Why? The Word says, *"Without the shedding of blood, there is no forgiveness of sin"* (Heb. 9:22).

Since it made no sense to send a dying Savior to rescue people who cannot die, God had no choice but to pronounce a death sentence over Adam and Eve. Otherwise, the only option available for humanity would have been the lake of fire.

How do we know this? All we need to do is see what the future holds for the fallen angels. If God could have sent a dying Savior for them, He might have saved them. But, because they cannot die, He has no choice but to toss all of them, including Satan, into the lake of fire, where they will burn forever.

So, as you can see, God had to make sure Adam and Eve would never again eat from the tree of life. By doing this, He preserved a people for himself who could die and live with Him for all eternity.

4

PROOF GOD SET UP ADAM AND EVE

"And Jesus, full of the Holy Spirit, returned from the Jordan and was led by the Spirit in the wilderness for forty days, being tempted by the devil."

LUKE 4:1

Now, you might say, "You have a nice theory, but it makes little sense for God to create Adam and then set him up to fail." You are right. It makes no sense to us. But for God, it made complete sense. Remember, He wanted people who could live with Him forever. If this meant sacrificing Adam and Eve to set His plan in motion, then there was nothing else He could do.

God knew a "Don't" command would set Adam up to fail by giving Satan an opening to tempt Adam. How do we know this? In Luke 4:1, we see God doing the same to Jesus. He had the Holy Spirit lead Jesus into the desert, where Satan tempted Him three times.

In Adam's case, God needed him to fail to preserve a people for Himself. As for Christ, He withstood Satan's temptations and corrected what he had done to Adam and Eve. He then stripped the old serpent of his power. Feeling defeated, this Demon left to fight another day, hoping to triumph over Jesus and keep his earthly kingdom (Luke 4:13).

SATAN WANTS TO KEEP HIS KINGDOM

Throughout history, Satan has remained focused on his effort to disrupt God's redemptive plan. I asked the Lord why. God responded by saying, "Lynn, Satan wants to keep his kingdom."

I thought, "Wow! The answer cannot be this simple." But, according to God, it is. Satan's yearning to keep his kingdom began with Adam, ran through Noah, landed in Bethlehem, showed up in the desert, and took place on the cross.

Now, if you think he will give up on the idea of reclaiming his kingdom, you would be mistaken. Let's not forget the tribulation period where he makes a military stance against Jesus and fails again (Rev. 19:19-20). Then, after Christ's Thousand-Year Reign, he tries again. And, he loses again for the final time (Rev. 20:7-9).

Observing Satan's effort to save his kingdom, he had to know about Christ's kingdom to come and his impending doom in the lake of fire. Every attempt to change his fate and keep his realm either failed or will fail. In the end, he will realize all his efforts were for naught against the King of kings and the Lord of lords.

BEATING SATAN—THE DESERT BATTLE

Satan's temptations always target one of the three sin categories: lust of the flesh, the lust of the eyes, and the pride of life (1 Jn. 2:16). He not only uses them against us, but he also deployed them to defeat Adam and Eve and tempt our Lord in the desert.

Where Adam and Eve failed, Jesus succeeded because He came to do the Father's will and not His own. Since Jesus had no sinful desire in Him, Satan's temptations failed to take Jesus down.

TAKING ON JESUS 3

"And he ate nothing during those days. And when they were ended, he was hungry." LUKE 4:2

Forty days without food left Jesus famished. Knowing this, Satan tempted Jesus to perform a miracle by turning a stone into bread. Instead of falling to the lust of the flesh, Jesus defeated Satan with the Word of God.

He said, "It is written, 'Man shall not live by bread alone'" (Luke 4:4). Where Eve failed, Jesus withstood Satan's effort to trip Him up, leaving him no choice but to try to derail Jesus again.

While Jesus faced down Satan's first temptation, this Demon was not about to give up. Instead, he chose the *lust of the eyes,* the same lure he used against Eve when she saw the fruit looked good to eat.

To deploy this temptation, Satan showed Jesus the kingdoms of this world. He then said, "To you I will give all this authority and their glory, for it has been delivered to me, and I give it to whom I will. If you, then, will worship me, it will all be yours" (Luke 4:5-7).

Jesus had no desire to circumvent His Father's plans by placing Himself under Satan's authority. After all, God cast Satan out of heaven because he wanted to be like the Most High. Now, he was at it again. This time his devious plan to seduce Jesus would have placed our Lord under Satan's authority.

To a normal man, the *lust of the eye's* temptation might have looked like an answer to prayer. After all, it meant Jesus could Reign without the pain and the delay to attain it.

But Jesus was no ordinary man. Wanting nothing to do with Satan, He once again withstood the temptation by saying, "It is written: 'You shall worship the Lord your God, and him only shall you serve'" (Luke 4:8).

When Satan tempted Eve with the *lust of the eyes*, she noticed how the fruit looked good to eat, and she eventually gave in and took a bite. On the other hand, Jesus withstood Satan's effort to entice Him to circumvent God's plan and place Himself under Satan's rule.

After failing twice, Satan selected his last weapon, *the pride of life,* to tempt Jesus. After all, it was his best weapon. It's the one Satan used to trip up Eve by letting her know she *could be like God, knowing good and evil.*

Having saved his best temptation for last, Satan took Jesus to the pinnacle of the temple where he said,

"If you are the Son of God, throw yourself down from here, for it is written, 'He will command his angels concerning you, to guard you,' and 'On their hands they will bear you up, lest you strike your foot against a stone.'" LUKE 4:9-11

Wanting no part of this, Jesus rebuffed Satan's third and final temptation by saying, "It is said, 'You shall not put the Lord your God to the test'" (Luke 4:12).

Where Eve fell to the temptation to *be like God,* Jesus rejected Satan's invitation to test God. And while Jesus withstood Satan's enticement, it would not be the last time these two would battle it out.

SATAN MISQUOTED THE SCRIPTURE

I find it ironic how Satan chose the words from Psalm 91:11-12 to tempt Jesus one last time. While he did not misquote these verses, as he did with Eve, he did leave out the words "in all ways." Psalm 91:11 says, "For he will command his angels concerning you to guard you in all ways." Meaning Jesus did not need to prove God's protection because His Father promised His angels would guard Him *in all ways*, including jumping off the pinnacle of the temple.

Having withstood Satan's best punches, the Word says, "And Jesus returned in the power of the Spirit to Galilee, and a report about him went out through all the surrounding country. And he taught in their synagogues, being glorified by all" (Luke 4:14-15).

What makes this passage an odd choice? Look at the verse following it. Psalm 91:13 says, "You will tread on the lion and the adder; the young lion and the serpent you will trample underfoot." This verse says our Lord will tread on the lion and the adder, the young lion, and who? The serpent.

Yes, Jesus will "trample him underfoot." With the entire Old Testament at his disposal, Satan chose two verses from a passage, highlighting Christ's victory over the serpent (Satan). Now, maybe you understand why I chuckled over his choice to use Psalm 91:11-12.

Knowing what Jesus had to face, verifies God's need for Adam and Eve to fail. Adam's failure made it possible for God to save a people for Himself. As for Jesus, His triumph over Satan, sin, and death, qualified Him as the faithful Redeemer who protects God's people from destruction. Adam and Eve's failure and the Lord's triumph both ended according to God's plan. Their trials made it possible for God to gain a people for Himself. And He would be their God, and they would be His people forever.

5

THE COVENANT

"And he said to him (Abram), 'I am the Lord who brought you out from Ur of the Chaldeans to give you this land to possess.' But he said, 'O Lord God, how am I to know that I shall possess it?'"

GENESIS 15:7-8

Abram, also known as Abraham, was a Chaldean. Though He knew nothing about the Jewish God, this did not prevent the Lord from calling him.

His story is one of faith. Think about it. While Abram's people knew nothing about God, the Lord chose to work through him and his family. By faith, Abram ended up following the God he had never known.

God reached out to Abram and told him about a plan He had for his life. This plan included a son for Abram and land to possess. He also shared how his offspring would become as plentiful as the stars in heaven. What else could a man receive? Overwhelmed, Abram needed some assurances from the Lord about the promises, and God obliged (Gen. 15:4-6).

WAS ABRAM'S QUESTION A LACK OF FAITH

"If any of you lacks wisdom, let him ask God, who gives generously to all without reproach, and it will be given him. But let him ask in faith, with no doubting, for the one who doubts is like a wave of the sea that is driven and

tossed by the wind. For that person must not suppose that he will receive anything from the Lord; he is a double-minded man, unstable in all his ways." JAMES 1:5-8

Now, some may wonder if Abram's need for God's assurance regarding his inheritance, may have shown a lack of faith on his part. The answer is, "No!"

God wants us to ask Him questions. It's not a lack of faith to do so. However, if Abram had doubted God's answer, this would have demonstrated a lack of faith. But he did not. Instead, Abram accepted God's response and was confident it would come to pass.

THE PROMISE GUARANTEED

"But he said, 'O Lord God, how am I to know that I shall possess it?' He said to him, 'Bring me a heifer three years old, a female goat three years old, a ram three years old, a turtledove, and a young pigeon.' And he brought him all these, cut them in half, and laid each half over against the other. But he did not cut the birds in half. And when birds of prey came down on the carcasses, Abram drove them away." GENESIS 15:8-11

Abram gathered the animals for the sacrifice and cut them in half by splitting them from head to tail, as was their custom in Chaldea. He then separated the animals and allowed the blood to flow between the halves. Later, Abram fell asleep.

While he slept, God appeared in the form of a smoking pot, and Jesus as a flaming lantern. Together, they walked through the blood between the haves and confirmed their offer to Abram.

No doubt, Abram understood what it meant to walk through the blood between the halves, for it was the way Chaldeans crafted an agreement. When Chaldeans made such an agreement by walking through the blood, they knew if one party failed to keep the terms of the agreement, then what happened to the animals would happen to them.

ABRAM HAD NO PART IN THIS COVENANT

As you can see, in this case, Abram had no part in this covenant, for it was a unilateral agreement where one party makes a promise, and the other party, who has nothing to do with it, receives the benefit.

For instance, when you purchase a new car, you obtain a warranty you had no part in creating or approving. Thus, you lack the authority to renegotiate the warranty's terms. Instead, all you can do is receive it as a gift for buying your new car.

Abram benefited from the covenant God and Jesus made when they walked together through the blood of the animals. If he had walked through the blood with them, this would have made it a bilateral agreement, where he would have had the right to negotiate the terms. But in this case, all he could do was receive what God the Father and the Son agreed to give him.

Just as Abram had zero input in preparing the covenant God offered him, we have no right to interject ourselves in the Lord's plan of salvation based on Christ's death, resurrection, and faith.

Like Abram, we are the beneficiaries of the two who walked through the blood. In doing this, they assured him that he would have a son, offspring more numerous than the stars, and land to possess. To receive his inheritance from God, all Abram had to do was accept it.

Moreover, in receiving God's assurance, Abram never asked God for additional proof, but he did suffer a minor lapse of faith when he thought Sarah was too old to give birth. For this reason, Sarah agreed to allow Hagar, her handmaiden, to lie down with Abram. In doing so, the two had a son named Ishmael. Even so, Ishmael was not the promised son.

However, 13 years after giving birth to Isaac, Sarah asked Abram to remove Hagar and Ishmael from their camp, and he carried out her wishes to remove them (Gen. 21:8-10).

GOD APPEARS TO ABRAM AGAIN

"When Abram was ninety-nine years old, the Lord appeared to him and said, 'I am God Almighty, walk before me faithfully and be blameless. Then I will make my covenant between me and you and will greatly increase your numbers.'" GENESIS 17:1-2

Once again, God appeared before Abram to update him on the promises He made. During their time together, God gave Abram a new name. He said, "Behold, my covenant is with you, and you shall be the father of a multitude of nations. No longer shall your name be called Abram, but your name shall be Abraham, for I have made you the father of a multitude of nations. I will make you exceedingly fruitful, and I will make you into nations, and kings shall come from you" (Gen. 17:4-6).

Because this was an everlasting covenant between God and Abram, God told him how he would become the father of many nations. Of course, this would take place through their Messiah, Jesus Christ.

Christ purchased us with His blood and grafted Gentile believers into Israel's branch, through Christ. By doing so, He fulfilled the promise given to Abraham about his offspring becoming more numerous than the stars. In speaking with Abraham, God reassured him of the covenant He and Jesus made, regarding his descendants, when they walked through the blood together.

Section II

THE PROMISE

*"God is not man, that he should lie,
or a son of man, that he should change his
mind. Has he said, and will he not do it?
Or has he spoken, and will he not fulfill it?"*

NUMBERS 23:19

6

THE PERFECT REDEEMER

"For the grace of God has appeared, bringing salvation for all people, training us to renounce ungodliness and worldly passions, and to live self-controlled, upright, and godly lives in the present age, waiting for our blessed hope, the appearing of the glory of our great God and Savior Jesus Christ, who gave himself for us to redeem us from all lawlessness and to purify for himself a people for his own possession who are zealous for good works."

TITUS 2:11-14

What makes Jesus the perfect Redeemer? We find the answer to this question in Leviticus. The Word says, "If a stranger or sojourner with you becomes rich, and your brother beside him becomes poor and sells himself to the stranger or sojourner with you or to a member of the stranger's clan, then after he is sold, he may be redeemed.'

As for redemption, 'one of his brothers may redeem him, or his uncle or his cousin may redeem him, or a close relative from his clan may redeem him. Or if he grows rich, he may redeem himself" (LEV. 25:47-49).

According to the preceding passage, a redeemer had to possess specific qualifications,

1. Must be a close relative.

2. Must have the ability to pay.

3. Must be willing to pay the price of redemption.

First, we know Jesus came to us in human form, making Him a near kinsman or close relative to us. And even though He faced Satan's temptations, Jesus never succumbed to them (Heb. 4:15). Next, because He never gave in, Jesus remained sinless, giving him the ability to pay for our sins, for the Word says, "Without the shedding of blood there is no forgiveness of sin" (Heb. 9:22).

The final qualification deals with one's willingness to redeem the poorer brother or sister. We see this play out in the book of Ruth. Boaz wanted to redeem Ruth and marry her, but he was not the nearest relative.

Knowing this, Boaz met with Ruth's closest relation to gauge his willingness to do it. Fortunately for Boaz, her next of kin declined, leaving an opening for him to step in and reclaim Ruth (Ruth 4:5-11).

Unlike Ruth's closest relative, Jesus paid the price for us even though He understood the gravity of His decision to become our Redeemer. Jesus knew He must suffer to pay the penalty for our sins and free us from Satan's grasp. Yet, our Lord never wavered.

Instead, He proved His willingness to pay the price by laying down His life to redeem a people to live with Him and the Father in the final kingdom for all eternity.

Besides the excruciating pain from the lashes and the Cross, Jesus also endured humiliation and separation from His Father while bearing the weight of all our sins. And even though Jesus asked His Father if there was another way, Christ never waited for an answer. Instead, He said, "Not my will but yours be done" (Luke 22:42).

In voicing these words, Jesus proved His willingness to lay down His life to redeem a people to live with He and His Father forever in the eternal kingdom.

And when He asked His Father if there was any other way, He knew the answer, because no animal or any other sacrifice could have accomplished what He did for us. By redeeming us, He returned us to our rightful family, the family of God.

In purchasing us with His blood, we received His grace, the Holy Spirit, a pardon for our sins, forgiveness, and eternal life. What more could we ask from Him? When we say He paid it all, like Abraham, we are confident He did.

7

THE NEED FOR REDEMPTION

"This is the book of the generations of Adam. When God created man, he made him in the likeness of God. Male and female he created them, and he blessed them and named them Man when they were created. When Adam had lived 130 years, he fathered a son in his own likeness, after his image, and named him Seth."

GENESIS 5:1-3

Past surveys show how most Christians believe we were born good, but our choices make us evil. A more recent Barna Group found 75% of the Christians surveyed "insisted that most people are good by nature."[1] Is this correct? Well, Genesis Chapter 5 offers us some insight into this question.

After Abel died and God banished Cain from his family, Eve gave birth to Seth. While God created Adam and Eve in His image and likeness, Seth, inherited his father's marred image and likeness of God. We know this because the Word says he inherited his father's image and likeness rather than God's image; the image Adam and Eve reflected before they sinned.

Because of his parents' sin, Seth, and the rest of us, inherited the same marred image. The only exception is Jesus. By placing our Lord in Mary's womb, God kept Him from inheriting Adam's sin nature. In other words, God made it so Jesus would have no chance of inheriting Adam's DNA.

UNDERSTANDING OUR SIN NATURE

Several years ago, an adult Sunday school class selected me to be one of their co-teachers. I felt honored because several of our class members taught at a local Bible college.

Regarding my first lesson, I chose to teach about the sin nature we inherited from Adam. While I had no idea this was so controversial, I was about to find it out the hard way.

As I explained why we inherited a sin nature from Adam, several adults stood and began screaming in my face. They let me know I was wrong because they believed babies are *born good*.

These people defended their position by telling me a baby cannot understand right from wrong. According to them, babies remain innocent until they know the difference and choose between the two.

Honestly, I was unprepared for such a reaction. I tried to calm my classmates down by using the Word to present my case; however, I sensed these adults were not interested in the truth. Hence, I gave up trying to convince them, and they gave up on me as their co-teacher. It was the first time I had endured such a reaction from those who were my brothers and sisters in Christ.

NEWBORNS AND THE SIN NATURE

Those who believe babies are born good may not understand the term *sin nature*. Having a sinful nature from birth does not mean God holds babies accountable for their sins. How could He? They have no concept of right and wrong. Even so, "We were by nature children of wrath, like the rest of mankind" (Eph. 2:3).

What does it mean to have a sinful nature? The word *Nature* is something that comes *naturally* or *effortlessly*.

While babies may appear innocent in our eyes, they are prone to sin from birth because they, like Seth, inherited Adam's nature, and not Christ's.

Consequently, we do not have to train our children to do the wrong thing, instead, the Bible says we are to "Train up a child in the way he should go; even when he is old he will not depart from it" (Prov. 22:6).

When a child is old enough to know better, the child, by nature, will choose to do the wrong thing. Thus, we are to train our children to behave. The training they receive will help keep them on the right path until they accept Christ as their Lord and Savior and inherit His sinless nature. When this happens, the desire to sin fades away as they continue to seek Him and His righteousness.

WE PARTICIPATED IN ADAM'S SIN

With this in mind, we can see why we need a Savior. After all, if we came into this world without a sin nature, then all we would have to do is teach our children to obey God's moral law. Then, they would not have to worry about Hell or the need to come to Christ because they would remain sinless until they break God's law and afterward receive their sinful nature.

As for Seth, he not only inherited Adam's sinful nature, he took part in his father's sin. Likewise, we are guilty of the same because we were in Adam's loin, just as Seth was in his father's loins. Similarly, we not only inherit Adam's sin, but you could say we participated in it. Hence, we were not "born good," as many believe.

"You might say, 'I am not even a hundred years old, so how could we have taken part in Adam's sin? Besides, he lived 6,000 years ago.'

Well, the Word says, *"One might even say that Levi himself, who receives tithes, paid tithes through Abraham, for he was still in the loins of his ancestor when Melchizedek met him"* (Heb. 7:9-12).

THE BIBLE DESCRIBES MELCHIZEDEK

"He is first, by translation of his name, king of righteousness, and then he is also king of Salem, that is, king of peace. He is without father or mother or genealogy, having neither beginning of days nor end of life, but resembling the Son of God he continues a priest forever." HEBREWS. 7:2-3

Jesus, after the order of Melchizedek, is our Priest forever (Heb. 7:17). So, when Abraham offered a tithe to Melchizedek, it was as if Levi tithed to him, even though Levi, who would receive tithes one day, was still in Abraham's loins (Heb. 7:9). Using this same thinking, we can see how we partook in Adam's sin.

Just as Levi was in Abraham's loins, we were in Adam's loins. And just as Levi shared in Abraham's tithe, we joined Adam in his sin. Thus, we inherited his nature from birth because we broke the command God gave to Adam by partaking in his rebellious act. And because of this, we inherited Adam's sinful nature the way Seth did, we humans have passed it down to every generation since Adam's offspring.

Now, what is interesting was Levi's and Abraham's relationship. He was not one of Abraham's sons, no, he was Jacob's son. Meaning he was Abraham's great, great, grandchild. And still, we can say, Levi was in Abraham's loins because He was born in his family line.

Likewise, while we are not Adam's son or daughter, we are in his family line. So, just as Levi was in Abraham's loins, we could say we were in Adam's loins. And because we were, we inherited Adam's sinful nature.

GOD CRUCIFIED OUR SIN NATURE

"We know that our old self was crucified with him in order that the body of sin might be brought to nothing, so that we

would no longer be enslaved to sin. For one who has died has been set free from sin." ROMANS 6:6-7

Because the law and our sinful nature are one, just as grace and Christ are one, we remained under the law's penalties until Christ crucified our sinful nature. In doing so, He set us free from the power of sin, which is the law (1 Cor. 15:56). Meaning, we no longer face condemnation under the law (Rom. 8:1).

Through Christ, God forgave us of our sins, justified us, and pronounced us not guilty by removing the law's jurisdiction over us. Now, instead of reflecting Adam's sinful nature, we bear the righteousness of Christ.

THE CONFLICT WITHIN

"Who will deliver me from this body of death? Thanks be to God through Jesus Christ our Lord! So then, I myself serve the law of God with my mind, but with my flesh I serve the law of sin." ROMANS 7:24-25

Jesus clothes us in His righteousness and fills us with His power to overcome our sinful desires through the indwelling of the Holy Spirit. While our flesh wants to continue in sin, our lust for evil vanishes because we have a new nature—the righteous character of Christ.

Paul illustrated this phenomenon by equating our desire to walk in righteousness to a man carrying around a dead body. In those days, if you murdered someone, your sentence might include having the victim's body chained to your back.

Over time, this dead, rotting body gets its revenge by decaying the murderer's body, leading to the killer's death. Paul said because of His new nature on the inside, sin's decay continued to infect His flesh, conflicting him with the righteousness he has in Christ.

You may wonder why some of our old desires remain with us after our new birth. Let's look at this from an earthly perspective.

Do you recall the 2010 Gulf oil spill? Who can forget seeing the vast amounts of oil leaking from BP's oil rig into the ocean? During this event, Louisiana's governor asked volunteers to assist in the oil spill cleanup along their coastal regions.

The problem was the volunteers had no chance to win this battle while the oil continued to leak into the ocean. However, once BP capped the spillage, this enabled the Louisiana volunteers to remove the remaining oil residue because they no longer had to compete with an active oil flow polluting their gulf.

Jesus did the same for us. By putting our sinful nature and the power of sin (the law) to death within us, we no longer see a "Don't" command as something impossible to keep. Instead, we view it as good and righteous.

In crucifying our old nature, Christ stopped the free flow of sin within us. Instead of seeking new ways to sin, the Spirit continues to cleanse our remaining unrighteous desires through *sanctification*. In doing so, we progress in our faith and holiness as God sets us free from our old desires, renews our minds on Christ, and transforms us from the inside out (Rom. 12:1-2). God made all this possible by crucifying our old self, which freed us from sin's power and placed us under His grace (Rom. 6:12-14).

8

THE REDEEMED

"For this is the will of my Father, that everyone who looks on the Son and believes in him should have eternal life, and I will raise him up on the last day."

JOHN 6:40

OPPOSING VIEWS

Who did Jesus have in mind when He died? Did He die for all sinners, or did He die for an elect people God appointed to salvation before the world's foundation? (Rev. 17:8).

We have two main opposing views regarding salvation. One is Calvinism, and the other is Arminianism. Calvin believed God predetermined those destined for salvation, while Arminius believed God wants everyone to have the opportunity to receive or reject the gospel of Christ. And these are the people God draws to Jesus. [2]

For whatever the reason, most believers side with Arminius. They believe Calvinism places restrictions on God's salvation plan, while Arminius' reliance on our free will to choose or deny Christ allows every person in the world the opportunity to receive or reject Christ's offer of salvation.

Those who agree with Arminius believe they have a much larger pool of potential believers. In contrast, Arminians feel Calvinism limits the number.

I am not sure Arminius ever implied he could add to the number of salvations. Instead, he limited God's salvation plan to those whom God foreknew would choose to place their faith in Jesus.

Calvin, on the other hand, believed God chose His followers before the foundation of the world. John 6:37 says, "All that the Father gives me will come to me, and whoever comes to me I will never cast out."

Do you see what I see? Those whom God predetermined and those He knew would agree to His offer of salvation must be the same people. Why? Because all whom the Father draws to Jesus come to Him. And No one can come to Jesus without the Father's drawing. By seeing salvation from a biblical perspective, neither man had an answer for those who reject Christ, or those who were never part of God's predetermined plan.

Because the Father must draw His people to Jesus, before salvation can occur; neither Arminianism nor Calvinism offer a way to increase the number beyond those God brings to Jesus.

God is sovereign over our salvation. Thus, He has no plan to add to His predetermined number to receive salvation (Rev. 17:8) or draw those He knows will reject Him because they, too, are the same people.

SETTING THE ARGUMENT ASIDE

The Lord has a plan to save His people, but until we see this plan from His perspective, the argument will continue. But, once we see it from God's point of view, we can stop crediting men's thoughts on the subject and, instead, credit God who designed the salvation plan.

The good news about God's plan is it never changes. It has a logical beginning with Adam, and a logical ending where the redeemed will live with Him forever.

You will see how consistent His vision is throughout the ages. By seeing it from God's perspective, the logic and simplicity of it may allow us to lay aside our differences regarding salvation.

Section III

THE PERSPECTIVE

"I will have mercy on whom I have mercy, and I will have compassion on whom I have compassion."

ROMANS 9:15

9

CREATING FALSE CONVERTS

"For by grace you have been saved through faith. And this is not your own doing; it is the gift of God, not a result of works, so that no one may boast."

EPHESIANS 2:8-9

Jesus never said our salvation relies on our human will or own doing. No, He clarified how salvation works by saying all the Father draws to Him come to Him. Therefore, when the Father, through the Holy Spirit, draws us to Jesus and enables us to understand the gospel message, we will come to Him in our need by grace through faith in His resurrection and His saving grace (Eph. 2:8-9).

The Lord makes it clear; without the Father's drawing, no one can come to Him. In contrast, those who make a profession of faith without the Father's involvement are false converts. Over the years, I have heard evangelists say only 5 to 10% of those who claim Christ, in this county, have experienced a true conversion.

Whether that statistic is accurate, I do not know. But what I do know is dealing with false converts in the body of Christ is nothing new.

False converts go back to the time of the apostles. And today, they continue because many, in the body, have presented a false gospel to willing recipients.

With this gospel, you never have to honor God in the way you live. Instead, you can choose Christ and live the way you want because Jesus loves you, and no one has the right to judge you since how you live your life is between you and God. Besides, you have grace, and God loves you.

My brother and I chatted on the Internet, years before My Space, and then Facebook came on the scene. We used to visit an atheist chat group where we shared the gospel with their members. There were times when they would tolerate us. And then there were visits where they showed little patience toward us and kicked us out, especially when we shared the gospel with them or stumped them with a question about creation.

What we found interesting about these Atheists is how most of them claimed they were once Christians. Yet, somewhere along the way, they became deluded and gave up their faith and replaced it with atheism supported by science.

I recall how we used to chat with a woman who was not like the others in the atheists' chat room. She was kind to us and always seemed tolerant of the gospel.

One thing I noticed about her is how she enjoyed hanging out in Christian chat rooms. So, one evening, I asked her why? She shared how she "used to be a Christian." I replied by saying, "There are no used to be Christians. If you were a Christian, walking away from your faith would make you miserable. If you were never a Christian, walking away would not bother you at all."

Several weeks later, to our surprise, she shared how she received Christ as her Savior. I was so excited to hear the good news of her salvation. And you could tell she was delighted to know her Savior, this time, for real.

After her conversion, she was all about Jesus. Yet, while she was happy with her newfound faith in Christ, her husband was not. She told us how he left her because of her faith in Christ.

After hearing her story, my brother and I prayed for her and her husband. Well, God answered our prayers. A few weeks later, she told us her husband had returned home after giving his life to Jesus. Yes, God reunited husband and wife in the body of Christ.

Many, like this woman, experience a false conversion, and over time become so disillusioned, they leave their faith. But, if God has destined them for salvation, He will not leave them in their lost state. Instead, He will reach out to them and draw them to Jesus, the same way He reached out to the couple who forsook atheism and returned to Christ.

CHARLES FINNEY'S FALSE GOSPEL MESSAGE

Charles Finney began his ministry in the burned-over district in New York, where people had grown tired of the many evangelistic efforts in their neighborhood. Finney introduced the community to a new form of evangelism based on one's choice rather than God's Sovereignty to choose those He wants to save.

As a former Puritan, Finney came to reject *election,* where God foreknew His people and embraced Arminianism. Finney believed people could change their eternal destiny by their free will. While you may agree with him, this belief would eventually lead him down a dark path, causing him to give up his evangelistic efforts.

Instead of relying on the Holy Spirit and the Word of God to change people's lives, Finney focused on attaining a "Yes!" from those in attendance. Based on the number of people who came forward during his evangelistic meetings, his plan seemed to work for the moment.

FINNEY ALSO LOST THE PURPOSE FOR THE CROSS

In addition to exchanging his Puritan beliefs for Arminianism, Finney lost sight of the real reason Christ died for our sins. From the Website, Got Questions, we read, "Charles Finney denied that we're born with a sinful nature inherited from Adam.

Instead, Finney said, our sinfulness is the result of moral choices made by everyone. Christ's death on the cross, according to Finney, was not a payment for sin as much as it was a demonstration that God was serious about keeping the law." [3]

If we overlook the purpose of Christ's sacrifice and deny the need to have the Holy Spirit's involvement in God's plan for salvation, we will end up drifting away from the truth, just as Finney did. Finney said, "While the Holy Spirit influences the decision, the choice to be saved is always man's"[4] In other words, he thought the human will could override the number of names listed in the Lamb's book of life.

RESULTS FOR DENYING TRUTH

According to those who witnessed these events, no matter where Finney spoke, a spiritual coldness came over those who said "Yes!" to Jesus. Instead of continuing in the love of Christ, they began to feel "burned out," and so they left their faith.

From the article, "Wolf in Sheep's Clothing," the author, Phillip R. Johnson, wrote the following about Finney's evangelistic results in the burned-over district in New York City: "Predictably, most of Finney's spiritual heirs lapsed into apostasy, Socinianism (a form of Unitarianism that denies the Trinity), mere moralism, cult-like perfectionism, and other related errors. In short, Finney's chief legacy was so much confusion and doctrinal compromise that Evangelical Christianity virtually disappeared from western New York in Finney's own "lifetime." [5a]

"Despite Finney's accounts of glorious 'revivals,' most of the vast region of New England where he held his revival campaigns fell into a permanent spiritual coldness during Finney's lifetime and more than a hundred years later still has not emerged from that malaise. This is directly owing to the influence of Finney and others who were simultaneously promoting similar ideas." [5b]

According to those who witnessed these events, no matter where Finney spoke, the results were the same. His false converts felt burned out and gave up their faith in Christ.

ONLY THE APPOINTED RECEIVE SALVATION

Paul and Barnabas headed to Pamphylia to deliver the gospel message to the Gentiles living there. Seeing the large crowds gathered around these two men, the Jewish leadership became jealous. Why? The Bible says, "When the Gentiles heard this (the good news), they began rejoicing and glorifying the word of the Lord, and as many as were appointed to eternal life believed" (Acts 13:48).

Appointed refers to "something decided beforehand or prearranged." With this definition in mind, only those whom God prearranged or decided on in advance, placed their faith in Christ. On the contrary, those whose names were missing from the book failed to respond to Paul's message given to those residing in Pamphylia.

MORE ON THE HUMAN WILL

"Regarding one's will, the Word says, 'But to all who did receive him, who believed in his name, he gave the right to become children of God, who were born, not of blood nor of the will of the flesh nor of the will of man, but of God.'" JOHN 1:12-13

The Apostle John had a close relationship with Christ. The Bible says he is the one Jesus loved. Knowing this about John, why do so many Christians ignore John 1:12-13, where he says the human will has nothing to do with salvation? After all, it's God who does the choosing. Still, most people believe we come to Christ through our free will.

If Finney was right, why did so many converts give up their faith? I am guessing the Father, through the Holy Spirit, was not involved in their salvation. Therefore, they would have been false converts who tried to enter the kingdom by using their free will.

Undoubtedly, Finney had a heart for people, and he wanted them to come to Christ by saying, "Yes!" to Jesus. However, as good as his intentions were, Finney's attempt to save people by their free will failed miserably. And instead of adding people to the kingdom of God, his efforts had the opposite effect. It caused people to feel so burned out they fell into apostasy.

THE DOCTRINE OF ELECTION

Besides what John wrote about salvation, Paul's thoughts regarding the doctrine of election, in Romans Chapter 9, support his writing. Paul points out how Esau, Isaac's firstborn, should have inherited the promise, but he failed to receive it because God chose Jacob to inherit the promise He gave to Abraham. To confirm this, the Bible quotes God as saying, "Jacob I loved, but Esau I hated."

"Even though they were not yet born and had done nothing either good or good or bad—in order that God's purpose of election might continue" (Rom.9:11).

As you can see, God bypassed Esau and chose Jacob to receive the inheritance. He did this, "so the purpose of election might continue."

Through Jacob's offspring, God put into motion what was necessary to fulfill the promise He gave to Abraham, according to His choosing, and no one else's.

The Word says our Heavenly Father picked Jacob so the purpose of *election* might continue. After explaining why Jacob would inherit the promise God made to Abraham, Paul used it to illustrate God's part in our salvation. He said, "So then it depends not on human will or exertion (work), but on God, who has mercy" (Rom. 9:16).

According to Paul, the doctrine of election is not about God's injustice but His mercy toward us. Paul said God is just because He creates both the righteous and the unrighteous to carry out His will and pleasure. He then reminds us how the Lord needs the Pharaoh-types to demonstrate His power and to make the Lord's name known throughout the world.

Likewise, the Lord requires the Moses-types to display His mercy. To reveal His glory, God hardens whom He wants, and He offers compassion to those He wants to receive it. Therefore, according to God's Word, our will plays no part in either of these positions (Rom. 9:15-18).

THE POTTER AND THE CLAY

Expecting a question regarding his illustration, Paul wrote, "You will say to me, 'Why does he still find fault? For who can resist His will?'" (Rom. 9:19).

In answering his question, Paul likens the doctrine of *election* to how a potter creates different items from the same clump of clay. In this illustration, God is the Potter, and we are His clay. As the Potter, God makes some vessels for a noble purpose and others for destruction because He needs both. Paul writes,

"What if God, desiring to show his wrath and to make known his power, has endured with much patience vessels of wrath prepared for destruction, to make known the riches of his glory for vessels of mercy, which he has prepared beforehand for glory—even us whom he has called, not from the Jews only but also from the Gentiles?" ROMANS 9:22-24

THE TWO CLASSES OF PEOPLE

God deals with two classes of people: The vessels He makes for destruction, and those He creates for mercy. Again, God never had the entire world in mind when He sacrificed His Son for us. No, He only had His vessels of mercy in mind; those He predestined for salvation. And while some might think this limits God's saving grace, we have no say in the matter.

As the clay, we cannot change what the Potter creates because we might disagree with His design or believe it places limits on our efforts to offer the gospel to everyone. Thankfully, salvation is not our work; it's the work of the Holy Spirit. All we can do is share the good news.

Through Christ, and the power of the Holy Spirit, God will draw those He chooses to save to Jesus. Our part, in this process, is to share the gospel to a lost and dying world, so those appointed to salvation will receive the good news with joy and gladness (John 6:37-39).

10

Jesus Left an Inheritance

"For a will takes effect only at death, since it is not in force as long as the one who made it (testator) is alive."

Hebrews 9:17

A person's legal will executes when the testator, the one who writes the will, dies. Being the testator, Jesus left an inheritance for His people. Like any will, it became available after His death and resurrection.

His gift to us includes forgiveness, grace, a pardon from punishment, justification, the indwelling of the Holy Spirit, gifts of the Spirit, and everlasting life. His legal will also contains an additional inheritance awaiting us when we become citizens of the new heaven and new earth. So, as you can see, there is a great deal at stake in the Lord's will for us.

In 2018, I served as the executor for a close relative's estate. By law, I had to carry out his final wishes according to his will. Since I had zero input in making his will, all I could do was notify his heirs and divide the inheritance according to his wishes.

A Will Names Specific Heirs

"For where a will is involved, the death of the one who made it (testator) must be established." Hebrews 9:16

Jesus knew His heirs by name and placed those names in His will. Who are His heirs? Revelation 17:8 says they are "the dwellers on earth whose names have not been written in the book of life from the foundation of the world will marvel to see the beast, because it was and is not and is to come."

We can see how this verse denotes the difference between Christ's heirs and the rest of the world. While the world will marvel at the beast, during the tribulation period, he will not deceive God's people because we are` aware of who He is from God's Word.

Those listed in the Lamb's book of life are the people for whom Jesus died. Again, if you are an Arminian, you might say, "This makes sense because they are the people who say 'Yes!' to Jesus." Or, if you are a Calvinist, you might say, "See, these are the same people God foreknew and draws to Jesus for salvation."

Regarding these two views on salvation, I have a question for you. Have you ever heard of anyone who selected their heirs based on those who will say "Yes!" to having their names included in the will?

For instance, if I had a hundred million dollars to give away, would I not give it to my wife, church, favorite charities, and children? Or would I say, "You know, I need to find out who wants some of my inheritance and include them in my will."

Who drafts a will this way? Logic tells me if we would not write one this way, why do we think Jesus would? So, I am guessing Jesus wrote His will the same way we do. In other words, God had specific names in mind (from the book of life), and He placed those names in His will before the foundation of the world.

Knowing this, what criteria did Jesus use to select His heirs? Well, Second Timothy 1:8-9 may hold the answer to this question. The Word says, "Therefore do not be ashamed of the testimony about our Lord, nor of me his prisoner, but share in suffering for the gospel by the power of God, who saved us and called us to a holy calling, not because of our works but because of his purpose and grace, which he gave us in Christ Jesus before the ages began."

Most testators choose family members to be their heirs. It appears Jesus selected His heirs the same way. Only those who were in Him, before the foundation of the world become His future adopted brothers and sisters. And this became clear, "through the appearing of our Savior Christ Jesus, who abolished death and brought life and immortality to light through the gospel" (2 Tim. 1:10).

THOSE IN CHRIST ARE HIS LEGAL HEIRS

By now, I know all this *in Adam* and *in Christ* talk may sound confusing to you. It was for me. And there are times when I still struggle with it. But knowing what I have learned, I am now seeing the end times from a different perspective. When I began to add logic to the truth, I eliminated what did not work, according to the Word, and kept what did. And this book reflects the latter.

God's Word refers to Jesus as the first fruit of those who have fallen asleep (1 Cor.15:20). Think of it this way. Because of Adam, all human beings have a death sentence hanging over them. Even so, Christ's death and resurrection set us free from our desire for sin, while the death curse remains on all who live without Christ.

Arising from the dead, Jesus became the first of the many who will overcome sin and death by receiving Him as their Lord and Savior.

To illustrate this, imagine I have an acorn in my hand. Rather than eat it, I decided to plant it. How many trees do you think my acorn will make? Logically, you might say it could produce one tree. And you would be right, but there is more we need to take into consideration.

You see, the tree from this acorn serves as the first fruit of many trees. Left untouched, this tree could produce hundreds of thousands of acorns throughout its lifetime. And each acorn has the same potential to produce more trees. So, my acorn could create, not one, but an unlimited number of trees.

But if I eat this acorn, instead of planting it, then what happens? Well, I would eliminate any future trees from this acorn, including all trees, they, and their offspring would have produced for generations to come. On the other hand, if I plant it, the tree from my acorn will serve as the first fruit of many trees, the same way our Lord became the first fruit of many in the faith.

By choosing to plant this acorn, it must first die and yield itself to a sprouting tree. In the same manner, when the Romans crucified our Lord and planted His dead body in the tomb, Jesus became the first fruit of all who are of the faith and will triumph over sin and death and remain with Him forever.

Executors Carry Out the Testator's Wishes "All that the Father gives me will come to me, and whoever comes to me I will never cast out." JOHN 6:37

God, the Father, is the legal Executor of His Son's will. Being His Son's Executor, He must carry out His wishes by notifying all heirs of their inheritance. Also, upon Christ's death, God cannot add any names to His Son's will after He died.

Just as a seed must die before it can sprout a tree, we, too, must die before we can have life. We experience this through our new birth in Christ.

What is the result? Paul describes what happens this way, "I have been crucified with Christ, and I no longer live, but Christ lives in me. The life I now live in the body, I live by faith in the Son of God, who loved me and gave himself for me" (Gal 2:20).

Again, only those the Father draws to Jesus are His inheritors. Those, He fails to notify will never receive an inheritance. Why? Because their names are not listed in His will.

Let me give you an example of how this works. When my father-in-law's mother died, she left an inheritance for her children. Her hired hand sued the children, explaining to the judge how my father-in-law's mother wanted him (the hired hand) to receive her farmland.

The judge heard the case and sided with the deceased's children. The hired hand walked away with nothing because he legally had two strikes against him before entering the courtroom. One, his name was not listed in the will. And the other, he was not a family member. Thus, he had no standing, so the judge ruled against him.

In John Chapter 6, some disciples, not the original Twelve, became offended by our Lord's instructions to eat of His flesh and drink of His blood. To express their feelings, they began to grumble.

While the Bible does not say why this offended them, I am sure they had visions of cannibalism dancing in their heads. Upon hearing their grumbling, Jesus said, "'The words that I have spoken to you are spirit and life. But there are some of you who do not believe. This is why I told you that no one can come to me unless it's granted him by the Father.' (For Jesus knew from the beginning who those were who did not believe, and who it was who would betray him)" (JOHN 6:63-64)

Jesus knew the identity of His disciples ahead of time. But these men, who had agreed to walk with Jesus, were not His. And for this reason, Jesus responded by saying, no one can come to Him, "unless it's granted him by the Father." So, the one who initiates the call is the one who exercises His will in the matter.

What this exchange illustrates is how impotent our human will is when it comes to salvation. These men chose to be with Jesus, but their human will could not change their legal standing any more than it could have altered the hired hand's standing. Knowing these men are false disciples, Jesus offers them a subtle reprimand, and what do they do? They walk away.

As I mentioned, executors cannot, of their own free will, discharge or add heirs to a legal will unless the law requires them to do so. For instance, you cannot leave a spouse out of a will in Florida. If you did, the state would override your wishes by adding your spouse's name to your will.

Regarding the Lord's will, there are no such exceptions, His Father will not add any names to the will, for God chose Christ's inheritors before the foundation of the world.

GOD USES EVERY MEANS POSSIBLE

I remember hearing a testimony from a man residing in a land where Christians were a rarity. Even so, God sent this man an angel to testify of Christ, and he received Christ as His Lord and Savior.

Like an earthly executor, God uses every means possible to locate Christ's heirs and inform them of their inheritance. When the angel reached out and shared the good news, this man received his Savior with joy and gladness; and it took place without any human intervention. Again, it shows how far God, the Father, will go to contact His Son's heirs.

ARE ALL NAMES LISTED IN THE BOOK OF LIFE?

If Jesus died for everyone, then every name would be in the Lamb's book of life. But this is not logical since people die and go to Hell every day, meaning God either failed to inform them, or they turned down the offer of salvation.

If you think about it, both scenarios are illogical because God must reach out to all of Christ's inheritors, and when He does, the Word says, "they come" (John 6:37).

Yes, when the Father gets involved with the gospel message, no one turns down His Son's offer. The likelihood of His heirs turning down the offer of salvation, or never hearing the gospel message before they die is slim. And even if it happens, the doctrine of election remains. We know this because John 6:39 says, "And this is the will of him who sent me, that I should lose nothing of all that he has given me, but raise it up on the last day."

If our names are in the Lamb's book, God has already given us to Jesus. However, we will not know this until God, through the Holy Spirit, notifies us of our inheritance.

Why? Because as the Executor, He must notify all legitimate heirs of their inheritance, no matter what it takes to do this. And Jesus must receive them and raise them on the last day; otherwise, some in the will would lose their inheritance, and if this were to happen, Jesus would have failed to carry out His Father's will. He, who carried out His Father's will and paid for these souls, would never allow this to happen.

So, again, we must ask ourselves this question, "Who turns down a legitimate inheritance?" I do not know anyone, do you? And even if one of His heirs initially says, "No!" to the offer of eternal life, Jesus will pursue the individual because He cannot lose any the Father gives Him. Instead, He must raise all, whose names are in the book of life, on the last day so they might live with the Lord and His Father, forever.

THE HOLY SPIRIT SECURES OUR INHERITANCE

"In him you also, when you heard the word of truth, the gospel of your salvation, and believed in him, were sealed with the promised Holy Spirit, who is the guarantee of our inheritance until we acquire possession of it, to the praise of his glory." EPHESIANS 1:13-14

Christ's legal will reads like a trust. Being His heirs, we inherit spiritual gifts, forgiveness, a pardon for our sins, eternal life, and the fruit of the Spirit. These gifts are useful for us to have on earth. However, we also have a future inheritance through Christ. The one I am talking about is the new heaven and earth. Like a trust, the Word says God has secured our future and guaranteed it through the Holy Spirit, making Him our guarantor until the day Christ welcomes us into the final kingdom.

Imagine you have a trust drawn up where if you and your spouse were to die at the same time, your only child would become the sole heir of your estate. But, instead of giving your child the full amount before he or she is old enough to manage it, you and your spouse assign a trustee to handle your estate. The trustee must keep the estate intact and distribute it to your heir according to the trust.

Thankfully, the Holy Spirit does the same for us? It's true. He is the down-payment on what God promised us in Christ Jesus. So, on the day we are to inherit the new heaven and earth, the Holy Spirit will make sure we receive it as spelled out in the Lord's will.

SALVATION IS THE FATHER'S PLAN

In John 6:38-39, Jesus says the plan of salvation was His Father's idea. Therefore, Christ's will must reflect His Father's plan.

While this is true, you might say, "Wait just a minute; I have seen people turn down the offer to receive eternal life. Would this not contradict what Jesus said?"

On the contrary, it proves the Word is true. Just because people hear the gospel and turn it down, this does not discount what Jesus said about salvation. I know, because in 1972, I rejected Christ because I thought only weak people needed Jesus. To me, He was some mystical crutch people used because they could not face life on their own.

Then, in 1985, God began drawing me to Jesus. I remember while driving home one afternoon, I heard this preacher, on my car radio, talk about the darkness in our hearts. For the first time, I realized I was not the "good person," I thought I was. Instead, I was a sinner in need of a remedy. So, I pulled over, parked my car, and wept before the Lord.

Several months later, I took a new job in Shreveport. Their new sales manager, Chuck Pyle, was a friend of mine. On the night I arrived at the radio station, Chuck met me at the door and asked me to follow him to his office.

There, behind a closed door, we had a chance to catch up on life and the radio business itself. Then, Chuck asked a question I was not expecting. He wanted to know if I was a Christian. Well, I told him I went to church, taught Sunday school, and read the Bible to justify why I felt I was a Christian.

After hearing me out, Chuck shared the gospel and how we are to have a personal relationship with Jesus. Recalling the darkness in my heart, I realized Jesus was the remedy I needed to heal my soul. So, on my first night in Shreveport, I received Christ as my Savior, and my life has never been the same.

What was the difference between my college experience, where I thought Jesus was a crutch for weak people, and this one? The difference-maker was the Father's drawing. God, the Father, through the Holy Spirit, drew me to Jesus by showing me the darkness in my heart. Not wanting to carry this burden any longer, I repented and gladly received Christ as my Lord and Savior. And, it has been my pleasure to serve Him ever since.

NO STRANGER TO CHRISTIAN PROGRAMS

During my college years and beyond, I listened to Christian radio and watched the *700 Club* on television. I remember Pat Robertson sharing the gospel each night, at the end of his television program. Plus, I know preachers and evangelists shared the gospel during their radio programs. Even so, without the Holy Spirit residing within me, there is no way I could understand what they were saying about salvation.

But in 1985, when the Father drew me to Christ, and the Spirit made it possible for me to hear and understand the good news, I received my inheritance with joy in my heart. Like a drowning swimmer, I grabbed hold of the truth and asked Jesus to rescue me from the darkness in my heart. And to this day, He continues to remove those old thoughts and desires by cleansing my mind through continuously cleansing my mind and heart of dead works.

I say all this because without Chuck's courage to witness, and the Father's tugging on my heart, I am not sure where I would be today. Yes, people turn down the gospel every day, but when the Father draws people to Jesus, "they come." Why? Because it takes the Holy Spirit and the Father's drawing to understand the gospel and receive Jesus as Lord and Savior.

11

A Deeper Look

At God's Love for All Sinners

"For God so loved the world,] that he gave his only Son, that whoever believes in him should not perish but have eternal life."

John 3:16

John 3:16 is the most recognized verse in the Bible. Believers use it to let the world know how much God loves everyone.

According to them, He gave His only begotten Son to offer salvation to every person in the world. And those who choose Christ will not perish but have eternal life. As for the others who reject the offer of salvation, they will spend their eternity swimming in the lake of fire.

To make their case, they think the term "world" (*kosmos*), in this verse, means sinners. In other words, they interpret John 3:16 to mean *God loves all sinners so much that He sent His Son to die for everyone.*

If this verse stood on its own, who could disagree with their interpretation? No question about it, we would say it speaks of God's love for everyone. But if you put John 3:16 in context with the rest of Chapter 3, we gain a different perspective.

For instance, John 3:18 says God has already condemned the lost who have rejected Christ. Meaning He is not pouring out His love on them. And for this reason, they already stand convicted.

Several years ago, my brother shared a vision from the Lord with me. In this vision, Lonnie saw himself sitting in a stadium watching a football game. While sitting there, he scanned the crowd and saw hundreds of smiling people cheering for their respective teams.

But as the vision unfolded, God began to peel off their skin. Horrified by what he saw, God told Lonnie, "When you peel away their flesh, they are like dead men walking. They have no idea they are on death row."

The phrase, "Dead men walking" is a saying that inmates use to describe prisoners on death row. While these prisoners remain alive, their death sentences continue to hang over them. Thus, the phrase "Dead men walking."

Another verse we need to review is John 3:36. It says, "Whoever believes in the Son has eternal life; whoever does not obey the Son shall not see life, but the wrath of God remains on him."

Again, as you can see, the above verse conflicts with the popular view regarding John 3:16. Now, I do want to make one thing clear about God's wrath and the condemnation awaiting those who have not received Christ as their Lord and Savior; John 3:18 and 36 do not apply to those of us who are listed in the Lamb's book of life.

Why? Because God reserves His wrath and condemnation for those whose names are not in the Lamb's book of life. Moreover, it would make no sense for His heirs to be on death row because they are His adopted children in waiting. Meaning, the Father's inheritance, for His children, includes spending eternity with Him.

The condemned are the dead men walking. They are those who do not have their names in the Lamb's book of life. The Word says the following about His sheep and those in waiting for the Lord to return: "For God did not appoint us to suffer wrath (Great White Throne Judgment) but to receive salvation through our Lord Jesus Christ" (1 Thes. 5:9).

THE WICKED ARE NOT IN THE BOOK OF LIFE

The Greek word for 'world' is the word *kosmos*. This word has several meanings: one is a group of sinners; another has to do with *organized societies* or what we might call *governments or nations*. It can also mean the *world* or *Gentiles or non-Jews*. And while there are several possibilities, the question becomes which definition fits with the rest of John Chapter 3?

For instance, if I substitute *nations* for *sinners*, in John 3:16, it not only supports *wrath, condemnation, mercy,* and *love,* it also corresponds with Christ's command to go into all the world and make disciples of all nations (Matt. 28:18).

God places His creation into two groups, *the wicked* and *the saints*. If we understand this, John 3:16 makes sense. As for the *saints,* they are the people God listed in the Lamb's book of life. On the other hand, the wicked are the people whose names are missing from His book. Below you will find some support for the existence of the two groups:

PSALM 10:13 says, *"Why does the wicked renounce God and say in his heart, 'You will not call to account?'"*

PSALM 11:5 says, *"The Lord tests the righteous, but his soul hates the wicked and the one who loves violence."*

PSALM 34:21 says, *"Affliction will slay the wicked, and those who hate the righteous will be condemned."*

PROVERBS 12:7 says, *"The wicked are overthrown and are no more, but the house of the righteous will stand."*

SOME FINAL THOUGHTS ABOUT JOHN 3:16

If John 3:16 referred to God's love for all sinners, where God makes way for every person in the world to receive or deny Christ, then we must assume everyone has their names written in the Lamb's book of life. But, this is not the case.

Why do I say this? I mention this because God placed Christ's heirs in His book before the foundation of the world. So, as I pointed out, not everyone has their name listed in the book of life. And Revelation 17:8 makes this distinction.

Revelation 17:8 makes a distinction between those whose names are in the book of life and those whose names are missing. Those who are listed in it will never face condemnation under the law. Regarding those whose names are missing from His book, they have a place reserved for them in the "blackness of darkness forever" (Jude 1:13).

LOVING THE LOST

So, how are we to love the lost? You may have heard of the phrase, "God loves the sinner but hates the sin." The original citation, "with love for mankind and hatred of sins," came from Augustine, not God. He wrote these words to instruct his nuns, who were debating Christian morality as it pertains to sinners, about how they should treat people in general. Augustine reminded them to love sinners but hate their sins.[6]

Centuries later, Mahatma Gandhi, India's Martin Luther King for the Hindus, who helped set his nation free from British rule through peaceful resistance, quoted Augustine by saying, "Hate the sin; love the sinner."[7]

Today, instead of attributing the quote to Augustine or Gandhi, people often attribute it to God. They say, "God loves the sinner but hates our sins." Or believers use this quote to describe how God loves everyone despite their sin-filled desires.

While the phrase sounds good, it's not in the Word. Even so, God commands us to love our enemies because we do not know who will receive life and who will remain condemned. God knows the difference. Therefore, we are to love the sinner, but hate the sin, just as Augustine suggested. For more on this, read Psalm 5:4

Section IV

THE PERPETUAL

"I will have mercy on whom I have mercy, and I will have compassion on whom I have compassion."

ROMANS 9:15

12

THE SHEEP

"I am the good shepherd. The good shepherd lays down his life for the sheep."

JOHN 10:11

While most Christians believe Jesus died for everyone, our Lord never said this. Instead, Jesus said He laid His life down for His sheep. Now, many Christians think we become His sheep when we receive Him as our Lord and Savior.

How could this be when the Word says His sheep hear His voice? Also, Second Peter 2:25 says we were like lost sheep looking for the Shepherd of our souls. With these in mind, there is no way we become His sheep when we receive Christ because we were like lost sheep looking for our Shepherd.

When we were without Christ, most of us made a mess of our lives. If you have ever looked back on the life you lived before Christ, chances are, like me, you have regrets. Why? Well, from Christ's perspective, we cannot believe how we conducted our lives through our high school and college years.

Back then, many of us knew we needed something or someone, but we did not know what or who? Some of us looked to different religions, friends, sex, alcohol, drugs, jobs, and our professors to find happiness, but nothing felt right.

Then, God began to draw us to Jesus. And for the first time, the gospel made sense. Because the Father, through the Holy Spirit, led us to Him, we knew He was the Shepherd we had been searching for but could never find until the Father drew us to Christ.

Once we received Christ, we stopped looking to other shepherds for answers. Instead, we pursued our one true Shepherd. And because of our faith in Him, we began to see life from a different perspective.

As we continued to grow in Christ, the Lord and the power of His Holy Spirit worked in unison to set us free from the bondage of sin. Along the way, we exchanged the dry pastures of this world with the necessary spiritual nourishment we need to satisfy our hunger for the truth. Yes, when God called, we answered because we knew His Son is the One who will never forsake us, despite the challenges we must face in this life.

THE SHEEP AMONG US

"I am the good Shepherd. I know my own and my own know me, just as the Father knows me and I know the Father; and I lay down my life for the sheep. And I have other sheep that are not of this fold. I must bring them also, and they will listen to my voice. So there will be one flock, one shepherd." JOHN 10:14-17

It's difficult to argue against predestination when Jesus said He knows His sheep, and His sheep know Him. Jesus also explained how He needed to bring His lost sheep into His fold. And in doing so, He willingly laid down His life for His sheep.

You Are Not My Sheep

Along the way, Jesus attracted some rogue sheep. An example of this took place after the Lord finished His "Good Shepherd" message. Some Jews approached Him and wanted to know if He was their Messiah. He said,

"I told you, and you do not believe. The works that I do in my Father's name bear witness about me, but you do not believe because you are not among my sheep. My sheep hear my voice, and I know them, and they follow me. I give them eternal life, and they will never perish, and no one will snatch them out of my hand. My Father, who has given them to me, is greater than all, and no one is able to snatch them out of the Father's hand. I and the Father are one."
John 10:25-30

Did you notice what I saw about his response? Jesus said His sheep hear His voice, and they follow Him. He then pointed out how His Father gave these sheep to Him, and they will never perish because no one can snatch them from His or the Father's hand.

In describing His sheep's characteristics, Jesus made it clear why these men were not His sheep. If they were, they would know Him because His sheep hear His voice. However, these men did not understand His message, nor did they recognize Him.

The Lord Knows His Sheep

Our Lord never has to wonder who His sheep are because He knows them. When they hear His voice, through the gospel message, they receive Him and follow the Shepherd of their souls.

You may say, "I still want to believe Jesus loves everyone." Well, in John 17, Jesus gives us some insight into His mission on earth. As Jesus prayed, he said, "I am praying for them. I am not praying for the world but for those whom you have given me, for they are yours" (John 17:9).

If Jesus came to save all sinners, why did He refuse to pray for the world? He refused to do so because He came to save His sheep, and not the whole world.

Knowing this, instead of praying for everyone on earth, Jesus prayed for His disciples and their spiritual offspring who come to Him after He ascends to His Father.

JESUS CHOSE HIS DISCIPLES

"Blessed be the God and Father of our Lord Jesus Christ, who has blessed us in Christ with every spiritual blessing in the heavenly places, even as he chose us in him before the foundation of the world, that we should be holy and blameless before him. In love he predestined us for adoption to himself as sons through Jesus Christ, according to the purpose of his will, to the praise of his glorious grace, with which he has blessed us in the Beloved." EPHESIANS 1:3-6

Both Paul and the original disciples had a similar experience. While Paul was not one of the original Twelve, Jesus taught him, using the same method he used to prepare the Twelve. He used the system know as the Beit Midrash.

Jesus walked with His original disciples for three years. Likewise, He spent three years teaching Paul in the desert. The three-year period was no coincidence because Jesus utilized the Beit Midrash system; the same method other rabbis used to train their students to become teachers. Today, the Beit Midrash is the Jewish rabbi seminary. [8]

Just as the rabbis hand-picked and tested their students to see if they qualified to become one of their disciples, the Lord, less the exam, hand-picked His disciples before time began.

Knowing this about Jesus and how our Lord chose His disciples, Paul explained why a person's calling originates with God.

He said, Are these adoptions based on their will? No, God predestined them "according to the purpose of His will, to the praise of His glorious grace" (Eph. 1:5-6).

Jesus had a similar discussion with the remaining eleven, after the Last Supper. He said the following, *"You did not choose me, but I chose you and appointed you that you should go and bear fruit and that your fruit should abide, so that whatever you ask the Father in my name, he may give it to you."* JOHN 15:16

GOD'S PLAN HAS ITS DETRACTORS

Previously, I stated how people want to believe everyone has a shot at salvation. I felt the same way, fourteen years ago. So, I get it. I know some of you have concerns about the doctrine of election—especially when we worry about our family member's salvation.

We want to think everyone has the free will to choose Christ. But, if God already knows who His saints are, then there is no doubt it would be a living nightmare to think about our loved ones dying without Christ because their names are not listed in His book of life. I get it. I had the same concerns about my family members.

PRAYING FOR THE LOST—A PERSONAL STORY

About 18 months before my father died, he accepted Christ as his Savior. My brother and I had prayed for him for years. My prayers always included these words, "God, please do not let him die without you."

It all began when I received a phone call from my brother-in-law. He told me the gangrene in my dad's feet had spread, and I should make plans to visit him as soon as possible.

Upon hearing the news, I flew into Orlando and then drove to the nursing home to visit Dad. While we talked, God gave me an opening to share the gospel again. But this time, Dad repented of his sins and received Christ; Twenty-five-years of prayer later, Dad received Christ.

When this happened, I could not contain my joy. All I wanted to do was thank the Lord for saving Dad. Excited about my dad's salvation, I could not wait to tell the rest of my family because they were worried about him and his salvation.

Did my dad have a true conversion? Well, I can honestly say I saw a change take place in him. While Dad let me pray for him, before he received Christ, he would ask me not to use the phrase "in Jesus' name." But after Christ became his Lord, he did not mind me using it. And, if I forgot to pray for him during one of my visits, he would say, "Lynn, are you going to pray for me?"

Well, after making several trips to Florida, I had Dad transported to Ridgeland, Mississippi, so I could keep a closer eye on him. As Dad's health continued to deteriorate, I prayed for him and wept before the Lord for his recovery. Even as I prayed, I knew death was closing in.

One evening, after spending a few hours with Dad, I received the dreaded call. The hospice representative told me, "Your dad passed away."

Returning home from Dad's funeral, I felt alone. Dad meant so much to me. We were as close as a father and son could be. Outside of Christ, he was the only other hero I had in my life.

As I entered my bedroom to change clothes, Satan hit me with these words, "He was not saved." Shaken, I collapsed on the bedroom floor and wept. After a few minutes, I staggered to my feet, grabbed my phone, and called my aunt, who was my mother's younger sister. I told her what I had heard, and she reminded me how Dad would never agree to something unless he believed in it. I said, "I know, and I am grateful. But if God had not saved him, I would be a mental case because I could not handle the horror of him dying without Christ."

Thankfully, after listening to my aunt's response, I came to my senses and praised God for having answered my prayers about saving Dad. After praying, my strength returned, and I have never doubted his salvation since then.

While we have no way of knowing who His chosen are before they come to Christ, God does. For this reason, God calls us to pray for the lost and share the good news with them. Even if it takes years before they come to Christ, we should never give up on them. If our friends or loved ones are His, our Heavenly Father will draw them to Jesus, so they can receive their Shepherd and live with Him forever, together, in one flock, just as He described in the parable of the "Good Shepherd."

Do you have loved ones who need salvation? Why not do what I did? Begin praying for them. Then continue praying until God answers it, and like me, you can rejoice in their salvation.

13

A TIME OF APOSTASY

"Don't let anyone deceive you in any way, for that day will not come until the rebellion occurs and the man of lawlessness is revealed, the man doomed to destruction. He will oppose and will exalt himself over everything that is called God or is worshiped, so that he sets himself up in God's temple, proclaiming himself to be God."

2 THESSALONIANS 2:3-4

As we move closer to the end of days, rebellion among the people within the church will occur. It's called Apostasy. When general lawlessness and apostasy increases, the Antichrist will reveal himself to the world. The Antichrist is the man Satan chooses to rule this world with an iron fist. His actions, during the final half of his seven-year reign, will terrorize the world unlike any before him.

The rebellion referenced in Second Thessalonians is twofold: One, lawlessness will increase all around us. Two, when these signs take place, those who identify themselves as Christians, but are not, will leave the church and turn to the Antichrist. These people will place their faith in their world leader. And when they do, because they knew the truth, they will be guilty of apostasy (treason against the kingdom of God).

THE ANTICHRIST'S APPEARANCE

The Bible tells us the Antichrist will appear when lawlessness abounds. And the church, mentioned in Second Timothy 4:3, will consist of people who "having itching ears, will accumulate for themselves teachers to suit their own passions."

We see this taking place today, especially in our churches, where denominations have split or considered splitting over issues involving God's Divine order. Members, who support these changes, often align themselves with pastors and other church leaders who purposely misinterpret God's Word to justify their wish to carry out these human sanctioned practices.

For instance, the United Methodist Church, having the second largest protestant membership, recently voted to split their denomination over the issue of gay marriage and the ordination of gay clergy. Expecting a majority to pass it, they did not anticipate the massive opposition they received from their international members. This global response caused the Methodist leadership to tighten their governing laws rather than divide their denomination. [9]

As we head closer to the appearance of the Antichrist, more churches will begin to accept the things of this world, as we continue down this path. We will soon reach a point of no return where lawlessness, leading to apostasy, within the church, will become the standard. When this happens, unbelievers will give up any pretense of looking to God for answers. Instead, they will place their faith and trust in the Antichrist. And when they do, the wrath of God will be upon them (John 3:36).

THE FALLING AWAY OF CHURCH LEADERSHIP

The Methodist Church is only one example of how the world's ideas have crept into the church. Today, we are beginning to see long-time teachers, pastors, and evangelists, leaving Christ and returning to atheism or becoming agnostics.

Were these people true converts, or were they pretenders? We do not know. But the truth is, Jesus will deal with their actions at the Great White Throne if they were never His.

From the website, "Alter Net," one of their stories showcases five former Christian leaders who gave up their faith and are now living their lives as atheists or agnostics. Some have even become outspoken voices for atheism.

Over the years, atheism has grown in this country. The Alter Net article mentions how one in five people, in the U. S., now refer to themselves as atheists. What is causing this to take place? [10]

Today many people, who identify as Christians, are leaving the faith and embracing atheism or another religion. Most were never Christ's in the first place. Instead, they were imposters who could no longer play the game. Then there are the real Christian apostates who, for some reason, lose their faith and look to the world for answers.

Is God causing fake believers to become restless, as we move closer to the end-times? If so, we could be witnessing the great divide between believers and unbelievers. While we may look alike, our hearts and our loyalties will be miles apart, much like we see taking place in our nation today.

While we may not know if God is causing them to leave the church, what we do know is this, the closer we move to the end-times, the more lawlessness will take place all around us, and apostasy will continue to increase. And as the Lord continues to glean the fake believers from the true church, we may soon find ourselves staring into the face of the Antichrist.

RELIGIOUS AFFILIATION DECLINING IN AMERICA
The Gallup Poll's Findings [11]

This Gallup Poll reveals some startling statistics about the state of the church in the United States. In 2000, 90% of all Americans had a religious affiliation. But this is no longer the case. Form 2016-2018, this number has dropped drastically to where only 70% of Americans have a religious affiliation.

In the 2000 study, one in ten Americans who had no religious preference attended church. The latest numbers find this figure slipping to 7% in the last three years.

Who makes up these numbers? Today, mostly older adults attend church. And many have died out since the year 2000. But the lower numbers still exist within the younger adult groups. Studies show only 42% of Millennials, on average, admit to attending church.

But they are not the only story. Traditionalists, born in 1945 or before, have slipped from 77% to 68%. Baby Boomers, born in 1946, have dropped from 67% to 57%. Generation X, born in 1965, has declined 8%, from 62% to 54%.

Church Closings [12]

While COVID 19 has forced most churches to close temporarily, the real story is about the number of permanent closings taking place in this country. The statistics are startling. Between 6,000 and 10,000 churches have closed their doors, each year, since 2018. With declining membership, these churches could no longer pay for their church building and everything else related to church operations.

What has contributed to the drastic number of church closings throughout our country? Some of the factors had to do with the way neighborhoods changed; others had to do with general church membership losses in general.

The Rise of Satanism [13]

The Daily Mail's article, "The Rise of Satanism, in America," focuses on the Satanic Temple and its growth throughout our country. According to the report, instead of concentrating on Satan, this church is about activism, diversity, and religious pluralism.

And while most are not worshiping the Devil, they are carrying out Satan's plan. According to the article, the Satanic temple focuses on reinterpreting the Bible. In other words, they seek teachers who will tickle their ears and reinterpret the Bible to support their ungodly activities and lifestyles, so they can feel good about what they are doing.

For instance, I remember listening to a teaching on gay marriage and how liberal preachers reinterpreted God's Word to support it.

The Word says, "Therefore a man shall leave his father and mother and hold fast to his wife, and the two shall become one flesh." This mystery is profound, and I am saying that it refers to Christ and the church. However, let each one of you love his wife as himself, and let the wife see that she respects her husband" (Eph. 5:31-33).

Their reinterpretation went something like this: Marriage, as defined by the Word of God, is the symbol of Christ and His church. It's not about a man and a woman getting married. Instead, it's about marriage itself. These liberal pastors declared marriage, alone, to be the symbol of Christ and His church.

An Example of One Who Walked Away [14]

A year ago, in May of 2019, Dave Gass, Pastor of a megachurch, Grace Family Fellowship in Pleasant Hill, Missouri, renounced His love for Christ and walked away from his faith for good.

The article explains how he had suffered years of doubts about his faith and circumstances in his life were such that he felt it was time to act upon them and renounce his faith. He also explained how his marriage was never the type he envisioned for himself. So, what caused him to give up his confidence in God? Was it his doubts, or was it the fact he was in an adulterous affair? We may never know; however, we do know if we leave the Lord and renounce our faith as he did, it can open us to a life of sin and possibly torment.

A STORY OF RESTORATION

In Chapter 18 of this book, I discuss the consequences of apostasy, so I will not cover them in this chapter. Still, I would like to share a story I read several years ago about a missionary to Africa whose wife died giving birth to their daughter. Filled with grief, the man decided to leave Africa and return home without his daughter.

Years later, his daughter tracked him down. What she saw shocked her. The apartment he lived in was full of beer cans strewn all over the floor. Her dad was a mess, and his countenance was one of sadness.

As they talked, she wanted to know why he left her behind. He told her how he renounced his faith because of his wife's death. He then shared how God had disappointed him. This man recalled his missionary days and how he led only one insignificant young man to Jesus. Admitting to feeling like a failure, and with his wife dead, this former missionary had become so distraught, he left the mission field and returned home. In doing so, this former missionary renounced his faith, got remarried, and had two children whom he raised as atheists.

Upon hearing the story, his daughter responded in a way I am sure he was not ready to hear or receive, but God broke through. She told him how this one insignificant boy is now her nation's top evangelist, a man who has led countless people to Christ.

After hearing her what she had to say, he repented, and God restored him. As for his children, they also received Christ.

Committing apostasy is an act of treason against our Lord. Even so, while we are here, we can turn from it and allow God to restore us, just as this man did. But know this, we see it gaining momentum here, and in European nations that were once the bastions of faith, known for their great revivals.

So, while America and other countries of European descent are seeing their church memberships decline, places like the Middle East, the Far East, and Africa have seen tremendous gains. Is this pattern God's plan for the nations, or did it just happen this way?

The truth is, all we know for sure is apostasy, in the form of atheism, and devil worship is on the rise, and when these take place, the lawless one, known as the Antichrist, will reveal himself. When lawlessness occurs, around the globe, we will enter the tribulation, where Christians will become public enemy number one, especially during the final 42 months of terror. Knowing about the evil that has taken place throughout history, it's hard to imagine the evil Antichrist has in mind for the Lord's saints.

Knowing this, we must ask ourselves if we are mentally, physically, and spiritually ready for such a time? The answer might be, how can anyone properly prepare for such a time? Thus, all we know is God calls us to faithfully persevere and endure if we want to experience all He has for us (Heb. 6:12).

The question is, will we be ready to face such a time?

14

The Rapture &
the Tribulation's Purpose

"For in those days there will be such tribulation as has not been from the beginning of the creation that God created until now, and never will be."

MARK 13:19

The tribulation will be like no other time in history. The ungodliness, along with the breakdown of God's divine laws for the nations, will place the world under the most tyrannical government ever. Its leader, commonly known as the Antichrist, will make people like Stalin, Hitler, Mao, and those ancient despots mentioned in the Bible, look like amateurs when it comes to ruling with an iron fist.

Like me, you may wonder if Christians will enter the tribulation period, or will God carry us away before it begins, as many believe. To find the answer, I asked God to help me understand what happens to us when the tribulation begins.

After praying and waiting for an answer, God finally spoke to me. He said, "Lynn, to understand the tribulation period, you must find its purpose. "The mysteries make up the forest, and the trees are the purposes for the tribulation. Find the trees, and you will have your answer." So, I began to search for the truth.

Currently, most Christians place their hope in a pre-tribulation rapture, where God carries His people away before the final seven years begin. Honestly, when you think about it, who would not want the pre-tribulation rapture to take place, where Jesus snatches us out of here before it begins? I mean, nobody, in their right minds, would choose to go through the terror awaiting us during the last 42 months of the tribulation. So, who can blame believers for wanting to place their hope in the timing of this rapture?

When you consider having to live through the tribulation, where the most wicked person in history will lead the entire world for seven years, it's mind-boggling, especially the last 42 months, of the seven years, called the Great Tribulation. During this period, people will experience countless suffering because no one will have the ability to buy or sell without taking the mark of the beast (666), as dictated by the Antichrist (Rev. 13:17).

In my research, I found how one views the timing of the rapture will affect the way we prepare for it. For instance, if we believe God catches us away before the tribulation, then there is no reason to get ready for such an event because we think we will not go through it. However, if, by chance, there is no pre-tribulation rapture, all bets are off. Instead, we will find ourselves unprepared to enter the most horrific time in human history.

Can you imagine what it might be like if we are still here when the Antichrist reveals himself and begins to lead the world? Second Peter 3:3-4 gives us a hint of how the world might react if this were to happen. He says, "Knowing this first, that there shall come in the last days scoffers, walking after their own lusts, And saying, Where is the promise of his coming? for since the fathers fell asleep, all things continue as they were from the beginning of the creation."

Yes, not only will they mock us, those who believed in the pre-tribulation rapture will lose hope, and possibly feel they were lied to by people they trusted. Again, all this could add to the great falling away.

TWO PURPOSES FOR THE TRIBULATION

Considering what might occur if the pre-tribulation rapture does not take place, inspired me to pray and seek God's Word for the truth. Upon completing my research, I found two purposes for the tribulation period. I ignored the mysteries the Lord called the forest, and instead, I spent my time looking for the trees. He called these the purposes for the tribulation.

Here is what I discovered, along with some secondary reasons that caused me to question the existence of a pre-tribulation rapture.

PURPOSE NUMBER 1: THE SALVATION OF THE JEWS

"The coming of the lawless one is by the activity of Satan with all power and false signs and wonders, and with all wicked deception for those who are perishing, because they refused to love the truth and so be saved. Therefore God sends them a strong delusion, so that they may believe what is false, in order that all may be condemned who did not believe the truth but had pleasure in unrighteousness." 2 THESSALONIANS 2:9-12

When the Antichrist appears on the scene, God gives the Gentiles, who reject the truth, a delusion or false narrative, where they will discard Christ and worship the beast. The Word says, "Lest you be wise in your own sight, I do not want you to be unaware of this mystery, brothers: a partial hardening has come upon Israel until the fullness of the Gentiles has come in" (Rom. 11:25).

Paul mentions a time when the Gentile salvation bucket becomes full. He calls it the fullness of the Gentiles. When the Antichrist reveals himself to the world, those Gentiles who refuse the truth (Christ) will worship the beast.

Once this happens, God turns His efforts toward the Jews, so they will receive their Messiah when Jesus returns to defeat the Antichrist's army. For the Word says, "And in this way all Israel will be saved, as it is written, 'The Deliverer will come from Zion, he will banish ungodliness from Jacob' and this will be my covenant with them when I take away their sins" (Rom. 11:26-27)

What does the fullness of the Gentiles mean? Think about it. Just as God hardened the Jews, except the elect, so He could bring mercy to the Gentiles, He will cause the Gentiles to experience a delusion where they will worship the beast. He does this to display His kindness toward the Jews. When the fullness takes place, Paul says, "all Israel will be saved."

PURPOSE NUMBER 2: THE ENDURANCE OF THE SAINTS

"If anyone is to go into captivity, into captivity they will go. If anyone is to be killed with the sword, with the sword they will be killed' This calls for patient endurance and faithfulness on the part of God's people." REVELATION 13:10

When we think about what believers must face during the Great Tribulation, is it any wonder why Jesus, the Revelator, calls for "patient endurance and faithfulness on the part of God's people." *Patience*, because we will need must wait on the Lord's return where He will rescue us and defeat the Antichrist, his false prophet, and his army. *Endurance*, so we will remain steadfast in the faith during this horrific time of suffering. And *Faith*, believing Christ remains in control whether we live or die.

Since the Antichrist's terror will extend to the four corners of the world, we cannot afford to become weak-kneed Christians. Instead, we must place our trust in Christ and allow the Holy Spirit to guide us and give us the patient endurance and faithfulness we will need to survive.

Yes, the Antichrist will be more frightening than all the tyrants who have ever lived, especially when he announces how no one can buy or sell without receiving his mark on their forehead or hand. After all, God's Word says the following about the mark and its dire effects on those who receive it. Revelation 13:16-18 says, "Also it causes all, both small and great, both rich and poor, both free and slave, to be marked on the right hand or the forehead, so that no one can buy or sell unless he has the mark, that is, the name of the beast or the number of its name. This calls for wisdom: let the one who has understanding calculate the number of the beast, for it's the number of a man, and his number is 666."

Living through such a time calls for perseverance because we will not have the ability to buy or sell without taking the mark of the beast. And it will take steadfastness when faced with the choice. If we receive it, God will judge us and toss us into the lake of fire for our treasonous acts against His kingdom.

Moreover, if we refuse to have the beast's mark, placed on our hand or forehead, God will honor our decision. However, by ignoring it, we will no longer be able to pay for food, clothing, transportation, shelter, or anything else. And, unless the Lord provides, we will remain in hiding, scrounging around for our next meal. And even if we have paper currency in our possession, we will have zero purchasing power during the last 42 months of this terrifying tribulation period because digital currency replaces it.

Besides having to take the mark, inflation will run wild. The Word says it will cost us a denarius to buy a quart of wheat or three quarts of barley (Rev. 6:6).

In those days, a denarius, valued at 20 cents today, was the daily wage for a laborer or a soldier. [15] As you can see, even if you could purchase something, the digital dollar will not buy much during the last days.

The Word says it will take a day's wage to pay for a quart of wheat or three quarts of barley, making it challenging for those who have the mark to make ends meet.

WHO MIGHT OFFER SUPPORT FOR CHRISTIANS?

Unable to buy or sell during the Great Tribulation, God's people will need help to stay alive. The question is, who will provide the support necessary for Christians to survive?

While I believe there is a strong possibility for the Lord's miraculous intervention, where He supplies His saints with the food they need, I have identified a group of people who may have the means and the freedom to support Christians throughout the last 42 months of the tribulation. Who are these people? They are the Jews.

Now, you may ask, why do I favor the Jews in this situation? I say this because the Prophet Ezekiel speaks of a battle around the time of the Great Tribulation, where Israel defeats an enemy, possibly a Russian coalition of Muslim countries, including Turkey. After the fight ends, the Antichrist makes a strong covenant with Israel. (Ezek. 38:18-23, 39:1-8, Daniel 9:27).

It appears this covenant may include a security pact for Israel. Unlike Christians, this could be the reason there is no mention of any Jewish martyrs in Revelation, until the end of the tribulation when the Antichrist encourages the Jews to rebuild their temple.

Upon completion, the Antichrist steps into it and declares himself to be god and orders the Jews to worship Him. But they reject the idea, so he retaliates by killing two-thirds of them.

Before this incident, the Antichrist may have used the covenant to gain the Jews' trust and to earn their favor. For this reason, he may not have required them to take the mark. I say this because when Christ returns, they become His saints. If they had received the mark, Jesus could not have saved them. Therefore, outside of God's help, the Jews may be the only people who will have the freedom and the means necessary to support Christians during the Great Tribulation.

Well, what about the unrighteous Gentiles, could they offer their support? Of course, anything is possible, but the Word says they hate the righteous, making them an unlikely candidate to provide any assistance (Rev. 12:13-17, Zech. 13:8-9, Rev. 9:13-15).[16]

After finishing their assignment, the angelic beings curse the world with plagues. The Word says, "But the rest of mankind, who were not killed by these plagues, did not repent of the works of their hands, that they should not worship demons, and idols of gold, silver, brass, stone, and wood, which can neither see nor hear nor walk. And they did not repent of their murders or their sorceries or their sexual immorality or their thefts." REVELATION 9:20-21

Nothing, not even a plague, will cause the deluded Gentiles to return to repent of their ways and turn back to God, for their misbelief will not allow them to switch their allegiance from the Antichrist to the real God.

IS THE TRIBULATION RAPTURE LOGICAL?

The question is a good one. Does it pass the logic test? How do the two purposes affect the pre-tribulation rapture? We know God calls the Great Tribulation a time for the saints to persevere.

With Jesus encouraging the saints to stand fast and remain faithful to Him, is it logical to believe He would offer such a command if His plan included removing His saints before the tribulation begins?

But you say, "While God removes His people, others will come to the Lord, during the tribulation, and they are the people who must display patient endurance, right? I mean, even if the Gentiles fail to turn to Him, the Jews will, according to what you said about God switching His focus from saving the Gentiles to rescuing the Jews. And besides, when God hardened the Jews' hearts, so He could offer the Gentiles mercy, some Jews continued to receive the Lord."

True! And this might cause you to wonder if the Gentiles could also receive Christ if they chose to do so.

We find the answer regarding the fullness of the Gentiles in Romans 11:7. It says, "What then? What the people of Israel sought so earnestly they did not obtain. The elect among them did, but the others were hardened."

The difference between the Jews and the Gentiles has to do with the *elect* exception. In other words, God hardened all the Jews, except His elect. However, the Gentiles' delusion does not allow for such an exemption. Why? Because their salvation bucket is full. Meaning all the elect, among the Gentiles, have already received salvation. Moreover, Revelation 13:8 says, "And all who dwell on the earth will worship it, everyone whose name has not been written before the foundation of the world in the book of life of the Lamb who was slain."

The Word is clear; everyone will worship the beast, except the *elect,* who have their names listed in the Lamb's book. What keeps God's elect from worshiping him? Does their willpower prevent them from doing this? No, they are the same as you and me. They will fear, and they will do what is necessary to survive.

Yet, instead of caving to the demands of the Antichrist, God's grace upholds His people, and in doing so, He will preserve them by preventing them from giving up their inheritance by taking the mark.

As for the Jews, their salvation takes place at the end of the tribulation when Christ revisits the earth. Their survivors will receive Yahshua (Jesus), but not until He comes back to defeat the Antichrist, his prophet, and his military machine (Zech. 12:10, Rom. 9:27-28, Rom. 11:25-27).

Do you see where Premillennialists fall short? God knows what His people will face during the tribulation. Realizing this, He expects us to confront their wickedness with patient endurance and faithfulness.

If we eliminate the unbelieving Gentiles and the Jews as candidates for salvation, then who would be left to carry out the call for patient endurance and faithfulness, if a pre-tribulation rapture takes place? Nobody! Knowing this should cause us to question the plausibility of such an event.

Therefore, logic tells us the only Christians who will go through the tribulation are those who were of the faith before it began. In other words, instead of Christ carrying us out of here, we will find ourselves entering the tribulation.

Knowing this, we must prepare for such a time because God expects us to honor Him, with patient endurance and faithfulness during this trying time. It's the only way we can make it through the tribulation or die in and honorable fashion.

Now, can see why God told me to seek the purpose, and I will have my answer? And when you apply logic to the Word, per His instructions, it all comes together. Unless I missed something, it appears the pre-tribulation rapture is a figment of our imagination.

RAISING THE SAINTS ON THE LAST DAY

- JOHN 6:40 *"For this is the will of my Father, that everyone who looks on the Son and believes in him should have eternal life, and I will raise him up on the last day."*

- JOHN 6:44 *"No one can come to me unless the Father who sent me draws him. And I will raise him up on the last day."*

- JOHN 11:24 *"Martha said to him, 'I know that he will rise again in the resurrection on the last day.'"*

- 1 THESSALONIANS 4:6 *"For the Lord himself will descend from heaven with a cry of command, with the voice of an archangel, and with the sound of the trumpet of God. And the dead in Christ will rise first."*

These scriptures offer some challenges for the Premillennialist's view. First, there is only one resurrection of the saints. According to John 6:40 and 44, it takes place on the last day. Next, how can the dead rise first if there are martyrs during the tribulation period. Meaning the dead will rise after God snatches away the living if there is a pre-tribulation rapture—something else to think about when considering it.

HE COMES AS A THIEF IN THE NIGHT

- *1* THESSALONIANS 5:2*: "For you yourselves are fully aware that the day of the Lord will come like a thief in the night."*

- 1 THESSALONIANS 5:3-4: *"While people are saying, 'There is peace and security,' then sudden destruction will come upon them as labor pains come upon a pregnant woman, and they will not escape. But you are not in darkness, brothers, for that day to surprise you like a thief."*

- 2 PETER 3:10: *But the day of the Lord will come as a thief in the night; in which the heavens will pass away with a* great noise, and the elements will be dissolved with fervent heat, and the earth and the works that are in it will be burned up."

- .REVELATION 3:3: *"If you will not wake up, I will come like a thief, and you will not know at what hour I will come against you."*

- REVELATION 16:15: *"Behold, I am coming like a thief."*

Returning like a thief, the Lord calls for the righteous to remain awake, so His return will not surprise us. As believers, we will know the season, but not the day. Not only will we see the signs, but if we have access to a calendar, it could help us pinpoint when the seventh year from when the Antichrist revealed himself to the world.

GATHERING OF THE SAINTS

MATTHEW 24:29-30: *"Immediately after the tribulation of those days the sun will be darkened, and the moon will not give its light, and the stars will fall from heaven, and the powers of the heavens will be shaken. Then will appear in heaven the sign of the Son of Man, and then all the tribes of the earth will mourn, and they will see the Son of Man coming on the clouds of heaven with power and great glory. And he will send out his angels with a loud trumpet call, and they will gather his elect from the four winds, from one end of heaven to the other."*

- MATTHEW 24:40 *"Then two men will be in the field; one will be taken and one left. Two women will be grinding at the mill; one will be taken and one left. Therefore, stay awake, for you do not know on what day your Lord is coming."*

In the above passages, Jesus speaks of a gathering that will take place near the end time. In Matthew 24:40, it talks about how two will be in the field; one remains, and the Lord carries the other away.

Regarding those taken away, I have heard some say this parable describes how "The Lord gathers His sheep and the goats to prepare them for the judgment of the nations, not a rapture." My guess is they may be looking to Matthew Chapter 13 for support.

After praying and seeking the Lord for some answers, I do not see how Matthew 24 aligns with the parable of the tares in Matthew 13:24-30. Why? Matthew 13 is not about the rapture, but the Great White Throne Judgment of the tares (the unredeemed) and the new heaven and new earth for the wheat (the redeemed).

In the parable of the tares, God allows the Just and the Unjust to grow together. It's difficult to tell them apart because they look similar. But at *harvest time,* or the day of the Lord when Jesus returns, a separation will take place. Christ will judge the wicked (tares) and reward His saints (wheat) with the new heaven and new earth (put in the barn) (Matt. 13:30).

SECOND PETER SUPPORTS MATTHEW 24

"But the day of the Lord will come like a thief, and then the heavens will pass away with a roar, and the heavenly bodies will be burned up and dissolved, and the earth and the works that are done on it will be exposed. But according to his promise we are waiting for new heavens and a new earth in which righteousness dwells." 2 PETER 3:10, 13

In these verses, we see how the coming of the Lord disturbs the entire universe and surprises the unsaved. Even though Jesus returns like a thief, He will not catch His people off guard.

Instead, the Word says the remaining population will mourn over the loss of Babylon, for in "one hour it was brought to ruin" (Rev. 18:19). And while the saints look forward to His coming, the others will see their world crumble before them (Rev. 18:11).

After the Lord returns and finishes judging the nations, Jesus begins His Thousand-Year Reign. Once the Millennial Kingdom ends, He will pronounce judgment on the unredeemed and toss them into the lake of fire. As for the redeemed, we will be with Him in the new heaven and new earth forever.

IT ALL HAPPENS AT ONCE

The Premillennialists have a difficult time seeing how the post-tribulation rapture works since the Lord would have to combine the snatching away of the saints with their immediate return in their glorified bodies. They say combining the two would make it difficult, if not impossible, to carry out both. But, as for me, I fail to see their concern, Why? Well, First Corinthians tells us how the Lord does it. The Word says, "In a moment, in the twinkling of an eye, at the last trumpet. For the trumpet will sound, and the dead will be raised imperishable, and we shall be changed" (1 Cor. 15:52).

What we see in this verse is how quickly the change takes place. The Lord rescues us on the last trumpet, just as Paul said it would happen. First, He raises the dead in their glorified bodies; then, in the twinkling of an eye, He does the same for the survivors.

After the transformation, we return with Christ, where He battles the Antichrist, the prophet, and their army. As to wondering if the rapture, change, and judgment of the nations can all take place at the end of the tribulation, it looks doable because we receive our glorified bodies in the "twinkling of an eye."

THE WEDDING

"Hallelujah! For the Lord our God the Almighty reigns. Let us rejoice and exult and give him the glory, or the marriage of the Lamb has come, and his Bride has made

herself ready; it was granted her to clothe herself with fine linen, bright and pure"— for the fine linen is the righteous deeds of the saints. And the angel said to me, "Write this: Blessed are those who are invited to the marriage supper of the Lamb." And he said to me, "These are the true words of God." REVELATION 19:6-9

I have tried to figure out the timing of the marriage between Christ and His church. The key to understanding this has to do with knowing the purpose of marriage. Marriage is a covenant between a man and a woman for life, where the two become one flesh. Marriage reflects the promise God gave to Abraham. And the fulfillment happens when Jesus and His Bride become one, for all eternity.

So, in trying to figure out how the Bride prepares for this wedding when Jesus has yet to defeat Satan's army and the nations who are enemies of Jerusalem, I believe I may have the answer. The wedding, in this case, takes place when Christ and His church become one.

It appears the marriage happens between the rapture when we receive our glorified bodies and sometime during His Reign over the Millennial Kingdom. And of course, the wedding feast will follow this event, based on the Jewish wedding tradition.

The Bride is ready for this wedding, clothed in fine linen described as the righteous deeds of the saints (Rev. 21:8). In v. 9, the Bible says the wedding feast invitations have gone out, and those who receive them are blessed because they are those who will live with Christ and His Father for eternity.

It's glorious how it all comes together, just as the Lord and His Father planned. The Lord had to make sure everything played out according to the script to create a people for Himself and His Son for all eternity.

Yes, over a six-thousand-year period, everything takes place on time. When you think about it, it's incredible. And it all culminates with the marriage and the wedding supper of the Lamb. Afterward, Jesus and His Bride will spend eternity together.

Although it's difficult to imagine what life will be like in our eternal kingdom, all we can do now is thank Him for wrapping us in His "Amazing grace."

FINAL COMMENTS ABOUT THE TRIBULATION

"For God has not destined us for wrath, but to obtain salvation through our Lord Jesus Christ," 1 THESSALONIANS 5:9

Most Premillennialists use this verse as justification for the pre-tribulation rapture. However, if being the Lord's saints means we will not have to suffer God's wrath on the earth, during the tribulation, then why do those who come after us need to endure the hardship? Are they not His saints, also? Moreover, should He not snatch them away, as well, to prevent them from experiencing the Lord's wrath during the tribulation period?

If the Premillennialists use v. 5:9 to prove the need for a pre-tribulation rapture, this truth must apply to all saints, not just those who were in Christ before it begins. Otherwise, it's not a universal truth, or the *wrath*, in this case, is not referring to the tribulation period, as many believe.

You see, suffering is part of our salvation experience. It's the one thing we can count on besides the Lord's love for us. The Word says we share in His suffering when we face it for doing what is right in God's eyes (1 Pet. 2:20-21).

Being a Christian does not exclude us from troubling times, whether on earth now, or during the tribulation period. Besides, the saints will face Satan's wrath rather than God's wrath during the Great Tribulation.

GOD'S UNIVERSAL PROTECTION FOR ALL SAINTS

Therefore, the wrath, in v. 5:9 points to God's eternal wrath, and not the tribulation period. As Christians, Christ's death, and resurrection, excludes us from facing condemnation and the Lord's fury at the Great White Throne Judgment seat. Instead of standing before Him, we have a pardon for our sins through Christ.

Rather than apply v. 5:9 to the tribulation period, God's pardon applies to all believers, including those who experience the tribulation.

Paul probably used v. 5:9 to encourage the saints. Think about it; the verses leading up to v. 5:9 spoke about the Great Tribulation. Understanding human nature, and how the knowledge of it might shake up the saints, Paul wanted them to know their ending is glorious. Unlike those who are of the Antichrist, we may suffer, but we will never face God's wrath at the Great White Throne Judgment seat of Christ.

A PERSONAL TESTIMONY ABOUT THE BOOK OF LIFE

"and all who dwell on the earth will worship it, everyone whose name has not been written before the foundation of the world in the book of life of the Lamb who was slain." REVELATION 13:8

One thing I feared about the Great Tribulation is the following: "Would I be able to withstand the pain and not give in and deny Christ?" This question haunted me for years until I came across v. 13:8.

Upon discovering this verse, I rejoiced to read where those listed in the Lamb's book of life, according to the Word, will not worship the beast because God will present them from doing so.

Instead, He gives us the grace, the patient endurance, and the faithfulness we will need to withstand everything the beast and his cronies will throw at us.

After reading v. 5:9, my fear about taking the mark left me; and I thanked the Lord for His love and how He will keep us from failing Him.

Of course, this promise does not prevent us from dying during the tribulation. It does, however, prevent us from denying our Lord and taking the mark. In our strength, we will fail. In the Lord's power, we will stand tall, no matter the consequences for doing such.

Reading Revelation 13:8, helped me to where I no longer need to fear the possibility of giving into the wrath of the Antichrist and losing my Lord forever. No, the Lord will remain with us; for His grace, power, mercy, and love will never let us fail. Will it be easy? No! Will it be painful? Yes! Will we stand firm in the Lord? Yes! Can we do this on our own? No! Not in our strength. But in Christ, all things are possible, even if we must die for our faith. Through it all, the Lord will reward us for our faithfulness.

And once He returns, we will remain with Him forever because this is the universal inheritance for all those throughout history, who were, or continue to abide in Christ. Amen!

15

THE THOUSAND-YEAR REIGN

"When the Son of Man comes in his glory, and all the angels with him, then he will sit on his glorious throne. Before him will be gathered all the nations, and he will separate people one from another as a shepherd separates the sheep from the goats. And he will place the sheep on his right, but the goats on the left. Then the King will say to those on his right, 'Come, you who are blessed by my Father, inherit the kingdom prepared for you from the foundation of the world.'"

MATTHEW 25:31-35

Before the Lord takes the throne and reigns over the Millennial Kingdom, Jesus must deal with the righteous and the wicked who survive the tribulation period. To accomplish this, He divides the people who served His saints (sheep) during the tribulation from the wicked (goats) who failed to help His people. Once He finishes separating them, the sheep enter the Millennial Kingdom, and the goats "go away into eternal punishment" (Matt. 25:46).

THOUGHTS ABOUT THE MILLENNIAL KINGDOM

The Word never says the Millennial Kingdom is for believers only. Unlike the new heaven and earth, reserved for those whose names are in the Lamb's book of life, this kingdom lacks the same restrictions, as you will see in this chapter.

THE PREMILLENNIALIST VIEW

The Premillennialists believe Jesus rescues His saints by carrying them away to heaven before the tribulation begins. If this happens, only those who supposedly come to Christ during the tribulation period will go through the horror of the Great Tribulation.

Likewise, the Premillennialists believe a pre-tribulation rapture will enable Christians, who survive the terror, to enter the Millennial Kingdom in their bodily form.

Moreover, according to the Premillennialists, the Millennial Kingdom proves the necessity of a pre-tribulation rapture because they believe Christian reproduction must take place during this kingdom.

Otherwise, if the catching away takes place after the tribulation, allowing all Christians to enter the Millennial Kingdom, in their glorified bodies, this will prevent Christians from having children during Christ's Thousand-Year Reign, as perceived by the Premillennialists. And this could create a problem for them.

WHO ENTERS THE MILLENNIAL KINGDOM?

Believing human procreation must take place, there are two questions we need to answer regarding this kingdom. One, we need to know who occupies this kingdom. And two, Do the Lord's people need to procreate during Christ's Rein?

In my quest for the truth, I searched the New Testament, Old Testament writings, and Jewish websites to see if Christians were the only people occupying the Millennial Kingdom.

After finishing my research, I discovered how some people enter this kingdom in bodily form, while others come in clothed in their glorified bodies. To find out who occupies this kingdom, let's begin with David.

KING DAVID SERVES AS A PRINCE

King David will rule with the Lord during the reign of Christ, even though he will not hold the title of king in this kingdom. He will serve as the Lord's *prince*. And Jesus, according to the scriptures, will function as both "King and the Lord their God." Yes, it appears both will rule over this kingdom; one will reign as King and the other as His prince. [17]

- **JEREMIAH 30:9** *"But they shall serve the LORD their God, and David their king, I will raise up unto them."*

- **EZEKIEL 34:23-24** *"And I will set up one shepherd over them, and he shall feed them, even my servant David; he shall feed them, and he shall be their shepherd. And I the LORD will be their God, and my servant David a prince among them; I the LORD have spoken it."*

- **Other verses** include references to David as the prince and Jesus as the Lord (Ezekiel 48:22, 46:18, 45:9-25, and 44:1-3. Plus, Isaiah 9:6-7).

OLD TESTAMENT SAINTS

"Although Christians believe that only those who knew Christ would take part in this resurrection, the Bible makes it clear that several Old Testament Saints 'looked forward' to a time when the Messiah would come. The prophets talked about it, Moses predicted it, and I am sure at least part of Israel believed in it" [18] (Zech. 6:12-13, Isa. 2:3).

OTHERS WHO WILL ENTER THE MILLENNIAL KINGDOM

- The tribulation martyrs will come to life and serve as priests with Christ during his Thousand-Year Reign (Rev. 20:6).

- It also includes those the Lord appoints as judges. He gives this authority to the Twelve Apostles, the original Eleven, less Judas, plus either Paul or Matthias will fill the twelfth seat (Matt. 19:28).

- The Lord, Jesus returns to Earth with His saints, after the Great Tribulation. We will all enter this kingdom with our glorified bodies. (1 Thes. 3:13)

- The Jews who came to Christ, after the rapture, will enter this kingdom with their earthly bodies because they came to Christ after Jesus carried His saints away, making procreation possible.

- Also, Gentiles from all nations will occupy the earth in their bodily form, making it possible for them to have children.

- During the Millennial Kingdom, several nations will rise against Jerusalem. Jesus, who descended from heaven to begin His Thousand-Year Reign, will defeat them. Regarding these and other countries throughout the world, they will continue to exist during the Millennial Kingdom. But Jesus will require them to join Him once a year during the "Feast of Booths" or suffer a drought (EZEK. 16:19).

DO PEOPLE LIVE FOR A THOUSAND YEARS?

"No more shall there be in it an infant who lives but a few days, or an old man who does not fill out his days, for the young man shall die a hundred years old, and the sinner a hundred years old shall be accursed." ISAIAH 65:20

I was among those who assumed the people who inhabited this kingdom, in their bodily form, would live for a thousand years. But, through my research, I found this was not the case.

However, by the end of His Thousand-Year Reign, Jesus will have defeated all authority and power on earth. Then, He makes ready to deliver up the kingdom and place it, and Himself under God, the Father once again.

Why will death continue to linger on during the Millennial Kingdom? The Word says, "The last enemy to be destroyed is death" (1 Cor. 15:26). Meaning death will continue until the Millennial Kingdom is over, and we enter the new heaven and new earth, where we will live with the Lord for eternity.

As for the others, whose names are missing from the Lamb's book of life, they will die and later stand before the Great White Throne Judgment seat of Christ. Upon finding them guilty, Jesus will have them tossed into the lake of fire, where they will remain forever.

Those who remain in their bodily form, during this kingdom, will have the ability to procreate. This first generation in the Millennial Kingdom and their children will have up to a 100-year lifespan. We have no idea if this means everyone will live for 100 years, in this kingdom, or if the number of years depends on their age when they enter the Millennial Kingdom. I am guessing it's the latter.

For instance, if they enter this kingdom at age 50, theoretically, they could tack on another 50 years. Plus, people will die during this period, so the 100-year mark is the average maximum lifespan during this kingdom, just as 70-80 years is the estimated lifespan, as stated in God's Word, even though people can live longer (Psalm 90:10).

CHRISTIAN PROCREATION, IS IT NECESSARY?

Since death takes place, procreation is a must during Christ's Reign. But is there any eternal purpose for the saints, who survived the tribulation, to produce children? None, I can see.

Why? Well, after the first generation dies out, their family line, for the next 900 years, will remain unredeemed. So, all Jesus can do is have them destroyed and judged before the Great White Throne.

And minus an eternal purpose, does it make sense for Christians to procreate, only to have their family tree destroyed? Something to consider when exploring the need for Christians to reproduce during this kingdom.

Although it may not make sense for Christians to enter this kingdom in their earthly bodies, to die and be separated from Christ for most of the Millennial Kingdom, some Christian procreation may take place during this kingdom. The Messianic-Jews, who entered the Millennial Kingdom in bodily form, may have the ability to birth children. If this happens, then they, and later their offspring will continue to procreate until the end of the Millennial Kingdom.

WILL SALVATIONS TAKE PLACE IN THIS KINGDOM?

Now some believe Christians will procreate and have children who will receive Christ as their Savior during this time. Regarding salvation, I have not seen any Biblical references addressing this issue. Plus, those listed in the Lamb's book life have already claimed their inheritance.

We know this because Gentile salvations ended, and Jews received their Messiah. And, as for the remaining saints, they received their new, glorified bodies during the rapture. Also, Christ's death covers both the living and the dead. Meaning, without another blood sacrifice, all salvations were accounted for before this kingdom began.

Therefore, since the Lord's legal will has already executed, He would have to die again and create a new, legal will to include people in this kingdom, for there must be a blood sacrifice to receive eternal forgiveness (Heb. 9:22). And this will not happen; after all, the Lamb is now King.

JESUS WILL RULE WITH A ROD OF IRON

"And the armies of heaven, arrayed in fine linen, white and pure, were following him on white horses. From his mouth comes a sharp sword with which to strike down

the nations, and he will rule them with a rod of iron."
REVELATION 19:14-15

Revelation 19:15 helps us understand who will occupy this kingdom in bodily form. During His Reign, the Lord will conquer His enemies. He will also rule this kingdom with a rod of iron. Now think about it, if Christians were the only people to occupy this kingdom, in bodily form, would there be any need for Jesus to rule with a rod of iron? Yet, He does rule this way; plus, He destroys His enemies because unredeemed Gentiles inhabit this kingdom.

Moreover, there will also be a time of peace when our Lord subdues His enemies. The Word says the lion and the lamb will lie together, and nations will no longer have military armaments. But individuals will have disputes, and so the twelve judges will handle them as they arise (Isa. 2:4, 11:6-9, Micah 4:1-3).

THE LORD SETS SATAN LOOSE

"And when the thousand years are ended, Satan will be released from his prison. He will come out to deceive the nations that are at the four corners of the earth, Gog and Magog, to gather them for battle; their number is like the sand of the sea. And they marched up over the broad plain of the earth and surrounded the camp of the saints and the beloved city, but fire came down from heaven and consumed them, and the devil who had deceived them was thrown into the lake of fire and sulfur where the beast and the false prophet were, and they will be tormented day and night forever and ever."
REVELATION 20:8-10

After a thousand years, Jesus allows Satan to run loose in the Millennial Kingdom. As you can see, he roams the earth and gathers all those who are unredeemed, the offspring, to "surround the camp of the saints and the beloved city."

Although God obliterates the unredeemed, the Lord will see them standing before Him at the Great White Throne Judgment seat. As for Satan, Jesus has him tossed into the lake of fire, along with the beast and the prophet, where they will "be tormented day and night, forever and ever."

Now, you might wonder what happened to these people, and how could they fall so quickly to Satan's temptation? Well, a few thoughts come to mind: First, these people were not redeemed. Some may have followed the Lord's teachings, but, as we discussed, they were never saved because Christ's sacrifice ended with the world, as we know it, ends.

Next, the further a nation, or in this case, a kingdom moves away from its founding principles, the more rebellious their later generations become. We see this taking place in our nation today. Generations Y and Z have been deprived of what this nation had to go through, so they might have the freedoms they enjoy today.

The same thing happened to ancient Israel. The further they moved from their desert experience, and what God did for them, the more they began to rebel against the Lord by worshiping idols.

During the thousand-year reign, several generations will come and go. Thus, the last one will have little in common with the first generation. Putting this into perspective, a thousand years ago, on this earth, knights fought for their kings in AD 1100, four hundred years before the Reformation takes place.

When looking at what took place a thousand years ago, and how we live today, we can see why the last generation, in the Millennial Kingdom, will have little understanding about how the Lord rescued His people from the Great tribulation. Nor will they have any idea about the enemies Jesus had to subdue to bring peace to this kingdom.

But when Satan comes, he tempts the unredeemed into following him. He would never be able to accomplish this if the people were not already thinking about rebelling. So God uses this gathering to eliminate the unredeemed before the Judgment begins, and He and His saints finally occupy the new heaven and new earth (James. 1:13-14).

THE TREE OF LIFE

"He who has an ear, let him hear what the Spirit says to the churches. 'To the one who conquers I will grant to eat of the tree of life, which is in the paradise of God.'" REVELATION 2:7

God blocked the tree of life, so Adam and Eve could not eat from it. However, in the new heaven and new earth, God's people will freely eat from the tree of life. Yet, in the Millennial Kingdom, John's vision does not include the tree of life.

Why? Because the unredeemed Gentiles and their offspring inhabit this kingdom. And just as God blocked the tree of life, to keep Adam and Eve from eating its fruit, there is no mention of this tree in the Millennial Kingdom because God cannot let the unredeemed to eat from this tree and live.

WHAT ABOUT AMILLENNIALISM?

You may be familiar with Amillennialism. Those who identify as Amillennialists use the Old Testament to prove the Millennial Kingdom is not literal. Instead, they believe it began when Jesus ascended to His Father.

Thus, they view this kingdom as an illustration of the church age from the Lord's ascension to His return after the Great Tribulation.

When it comes to Amillennialism, I have no problem with this point of view. Some well-respected Theologians adhere to it. Then, there is the opposite view held by the Premillennialists. Again, this group is also represented by some well-respected Theologians. The Premillennialists believe this kingdom will take place, as the Word describes, and Jesus will rule over it, as the Bible states.

So, I agree with the Amillennialists about the rapture taking place after the Great Tribulation. Also, I align with the Premillennialists, who believe in a literal Thousand-Year Reign. Again, this kingdom, in their minds, proves the need for a pretribulation rapture, so Christians may enter this kingdom in their bodily form. And give birth.

MY CONCERN ABOUT AMILLENNIALISM

- First, I find it difficult to believe the Lord needs to illustrate His reign from heaven by creating a kingdom that will never exist. It makes no sense.

- Second, Jesus died on the cross and ascended to the Father, after carrying out His Father's plans to the fullest. If this was my Son, and I am well pleased with Him, why not reward Him with a kingdom He can rule over for a thousand years? Besides, this kingdom would allow Jesus and the saints to get to know each other personally.

- Third, the Old Testament does give us insight into the reality of this kingdom.

- Fourth, if this is not a literal kingdom, then why place a 100-year lifespan on those who live in bodily form?

- Fifth, have you ever heard of a time when armies disbanded, and they turned their armaments into plowshares?

- Sixth, has Jerusalem's enemies made peace with them?

- And finally, have you ever heard or read about lions and lambs lying down together?

SEEING BOTH SIDES OF THE ARGUMENT

I rarely come from an I believe point of view in the books I have authored. Why? Because, for me, it's all about what the Word says and not what I believe. Besides, my concern about Amillennialists' position has nothing to do with their opinions, nor is it personal. Therefore, I will make an exception and let you know why I believe in the literal view and not the illustrative view held by them.

To begin, I agree with the literal view because it makes sense for the reasons I have already explained.

Next, if I thought this kingdom was nothing but an illustration of Christ's rule, beginning with His ascension, then I take the chance of dishonoring Him by not recognizing His kingdom to come, where He will rule and reign for a thousand years.

The final reason has to with the warning given to us in Chapter 22 of Revelation. In this chapter, Jesus spells out the consequences for adding to or deleting from this book. The Word says that we could suffer all the tribulation plagues if we add to Revelation. But if we discount or take away something from this book while teaching it, we could lose our place in the New Jerusalem. Plus, we will not be allowed to eat from the tree of life.

Finally, the King James version says God will write our names out of the Book of Life. Now, you see why I am cautious about discounting the Millennial Kingdom because it could have eternal consequences for those who adhere to this idea about Christ's 1,000-year reign.

Thus, I would rather error on the literal side, than take the chance of purging the literal view of this kingdom by aligning with the Amillennialists.

THE MILLENNIAL KINGDOM SUMMARY

It's interesting how I align with the Premillennialists' view about having a literal, Millennial Kingdom and side with the Amillennialists' where the rapture takes place after the Great Tribulation. I am probably in the minority, but it does not matter. Again, I never adopt unfamiliar passages from others without studying them for myself. I want to make sure what I hear or read is the Word and not someone's opinion. As for me, the Word provides the evidence (Old Testament and New) to believe in the future, Millennial Kingdom.

If you want to find out more about this kingdom, I suggest you start with the verses I listed on the next page. You will find several new scriptures to review. Plus, you can learn more about this kingdom by visiting Jewish websites and the Old Testament prophets.

ADDITIONAL SCRIPTURES FOR THE MILLENNIAL KINGDOM		
Romans 6:12	1 Corinthians 15:22-25	1 Thessalonians. 4:16-17
Zechariah 14:9	Daniel 2:24	Zechariah 14:15-24
Matthew 19:28	Luke 22:29-30	1 Corinthians 6:22
Romans 8:17	Micah 5:2	Jeremiah 3:9,17
Ezekiel 36:24	Revelation 2:10	Revelation 6:4-6
Ezekiel 38:1-4	Zephaniah 3:8-23	Micah 4:1-3
Isaiah 11:6-9	Isaiah 2:2-4	Isaiah 65:25

16

THE FINAL KINGDOM

"Then I saw a new heaven and a new earth, for the first heaven and the first earth had passed away, and the sea was no more. And I saw the holy city, new Jerusalem, coming down out of heaven from God, prepared as a bride adorned for her husband."

REVELATION 21:1-2

T he new heaven and earth is God's final home for the redeemed; those who conquered life and gave their all to Christ. As for Christ's rule over the Millennial Kingdom, it ends. It's difficult to imagine what the new Jerusalem will look like as it comes down from heaven. Its dimensions form a cube, stretching 12,000 stadia (1,400 miles) in every direction (Rev. 21:16). If God placed this city in America, it would stretch from the Mexican border to Wichita in width. Its length would extend from Houston to San Diego. And its height would measure the same distance or 1,400 miles.

What if we lived on the top floor of this enormous city and had to rely on elevators to get us to the top, would we need to pack several days' worth of food and a sleeping bag on our way to the top, or, would our glorified bodies allow us to just show up on the top floor? Anyway, it will be interesting, especially if you are like me and have a fear of heights.

"In my Father's house are many rooms. If it were not so, would I have told you that I go to prepare a place for you?"
JOHN 14:2

In John 14:2, the King James Version, says our Father's house has many mansions, while the English Standard Version replaces *mansions* with the word *rooms*.

Today, a mansion has at least twenty-five rooms, but in those days, the words *mansion* and *room* were synonymous. So, it appears the Father's house has enough rooms for each of us to occupy.

QUALIFICATIONS FOR THE NEW HEAVEN AND EARTH

"The one who conquers will have this heritage, and I will be his God, and he will be my son. But as for the cowardly, the faithless, the detestable, as for murderers, the sexually immoral, sorcerers, idolaters, and all liars, their portion will be in the lake that burns with fire and sulfur, which is the second death." REVELATION 21:7-8

Unlike the Millennial Kingdom, only the redeemed will inhabit the new heaven and earth. Liars, murderers, the sexually immoral, sorcerers, the cowardly, and the rest of the unredeemed will have no part in this kingdom. Instead, those who conquered, through Christ, will inherit the new heaven and earth, the realm God planned for us before the world began.

"But nothing unclean will ever enter it, nor anyone who does what is detestable or false, but only those who are written in the Lamb's book of life." REVELATION 21:7

Guess what? Your eternal inheritance is your big payday. No longer will you struggle with your conscience to do what is right. With the demons in the lake of fire, we will never have to deal with their temptations, accusations, or the lies they fed us anymore. No, God has made it so we can enjoy Him and the new heaven and earth without heartache or sin because only those written in the Lamb's book, will join us in this final kingdom.

THE TREE OF LIFE IS AVAILABLE TO ALL

"...on either side of the river, the tree of life with its twelve kinds of fruit, yielding its fruit each month. The leaves of the tree were for the healing of the nations." REVELATION 22:2

People from all nations will freely eat of this tree. Unlike the former Earth and the Millennial Kingdom, the tree of life runs on each side of the river, making it easy for people to access.

Why is this? Well, since sin and death are no more, the Devil and the rest of the demons are gone, and the unredeemed are swimming in the lake of fire, God no longer needs to keep this tree hidden or guarded. Instead, it's out in the open where the redeemed can partake of its fruit forever.

JESUS IS COMING SOON

"I am coming soon, bringing my recompense (rewards) with me, to repay each one for what he has done." REVELATION 22:12

Jesus will be here before we know it, and He will bring the rewards He has for us. And while we may not know the exact day, He will arrive. Even so, we can be sure the present days are winding down. No doubt, lawlessness abounds, and before we know it, the world will become one under the man the Bible calls the Antichrist.

We also need to be careful about how we share and teach Revelation. After all, we do not want to take the chance of forfeiting our future with Christ.

The question is, are you ready? Will you look for Jesus to take us out of here, or will you prepare yourself mentally, physically, and spiritually for such a time? In other words, you, and the rest of us, will need to be ready to endure with faith and patience, the overwhelming darkness that will rule the world with an iron fist for seven, long, years.

17

JUDGMENT AND THE LAKE OF FIRE

"And the devil, who deceived them, was thrown into the lake of burning sulfur, where the beast and the false prophet had been thrown. They will be tormented day and night forever and ever."

REVELATION 20:10

Many believe the final resting place for evil is hell, but it's not. There is a place more horrific than hell if this is possible. The Bible calls it the "lake of fire." This lake is the eternal place of torment for Satan, the fallen angels, and all the unredeemed.

Instead of a lake filled with water, heat transforms burning sulfur into a lava-like lake of fire that will burn forever. When heated, this rock produces a familiar blue flame like a water heater's pilot light.

Unlike a burning red flame, this flame is incapable of lighting up an area. Surrounded by the gloom of darkness, all the condemned will ever see is this blue flame dancing atop a sulfur-filled lake, the Bible calls the lake of fire. [19]

SULFUR'S CHARACTERISTICS

How hot will this lava-like lake get? While the Bible does not tell us, sulfur has a boiling point of 830 degrees Fahrenheit. And if all this is not severe enough, burning sulfur emits a rotten, egg-like smell.

With zero oxygen to breathe, those who suffer in this hot, waxy, lava-lake, will spend eternity burning and gasping for one deep breath that will elude them forever.

As horrifying as this sounds, there is more. Since the blue flame, dancing atop the sulfur, does nothing to light the surrounding area, the condemned will never again see a smiling face, hear a burst of infectious laughter above the screams, or feel a comforting touch from a loved one. No, instead, the condemned will spend their eternity alone, in pain, and gasping for air, all the while knowing there is no pardon awaiting them in the future.

Studies show when a person remains isolated from others for long periods, this can cause both physical and mental problems for the condemned. [20] And since they still have their earthly bodies, they will hunger and thirst, but no food or water will be available to satisfy their needs. They will long for sleep or companionship, but the pain, hunger, thirst, smell, and the gasping for air will deny them the comfort they seek.

So, count yourself blessed to have your name listed in His book of life. A blessing we should never take for granted. Instead, we ought to honor Him with our lives, while we still can, by choosing to live worthy of His sacrifice.

ANOTHER WHAT-IF FANTASY

"And I saw the dead, great and small, standing before the throne, and books were opened. Another book was opened, which is the book of life. The dead were judged according to what they had done as recorded in the books."
REVELATION 20:12

Let's play the what-if scenario one more time. This fantasy takes place at the end of the Millennial Kingdom, during the Great White Throne Judgment of the wicked. In it, I see myself standing stone-faced before the throne as the Lord charges me with every evil thought, gossip, and sinful act I ever committed.

While the embarrassing charges continue to roll off the Lord's tongue, I cannot believe how terrible I was. Back then, I used to compare myself to Hitler. In my mind, he personified evil, not me. Compared to him, I thought I was a good person because I had not murdered anybody. But now, hearing Jesus read the accusations against me, I cannot believe how naïve I was regarding the sins I committed and my need for a Savior.

Suddenly, my attention shifts to the present as my mind cries out, "Please stop! I don't want to hear anymore." Yet, the charges continue.

Seeing His radiant splendor oozing from Him, I kneel before Jesus, hoping He would take pity on me, but it does not work. Whatever hope I had in saving myself from the fire soon fades away.

Having failed to gain His sympathy, Jesus orders me to stand. Struggling to get off my aching knees, I now realize how foolish it was for me to ignore my Christian friends' warnings about my future without Christ. Back then, I thought they were just trying to scare me. How foolish of me to believe only weak people need Jesus.

Claiming they had the truth, I told my friends, "It may be true for you, but it's not true for me." Oh, if only I had listened, I would not be standing in front of Jesus today. But here I am, quaking before the real Jesus as He sits on His Great White Throne, reading all the endless charges against me.

Looking back, I now realize my friends were right. I was the one who was living a lie by refusing to forsake the pleasures of this world. And because of my ignorance, the lake of fire will be my forever destination.

With tears rolling slowly down my cheeks, the thought of my destination terrifies me. I deeply regret how I lived my life. But it's too late for regrets, for I cannot change my destiny.

Finally, the charges end. Without any hesitation, Jesus motions for His angels to grab me and toss me into the lake. As they drag me away, I dig my heels into the ground, hoping to delay them, but it was a useless effort on my part.

Now, standing at the edge of the abyss, I turn my head and yell, "Jesus, where is your mercy?" Without a hint of sympathy from Him, Jesus declares, "I left it on the cross."

With my heart pounding, I cry out, "No! No!" Then, they release me into the dark abyss. As I sail down, I look around for something to grab onto, to keep me from my destiny. But all I see are the bloodied, jagged walls that testify of the futile efforts of others who tried to stall their descent by digging their fingers into the rough surroundings.

Seeing the dancing blue flames approach, I hear a chorus of screams echoing off the sides of the abyss. Nearing the end of my downward journey, I brace myself for the worst as I splash into the molten lava-like lake of fire.

While sinking, the boiling heat sends shocks through me as the waxy sulfur engulfs me and inflames every nerve in my body. Without thinking, I join the chorus and cry out, knowing there is no one to rescue me.

No matter how disturbing I imagined it would be, nothing prepared me for this. It's much worse than anything I could have conjured up in my mind.

As I try to stay focused amidst the screams and the pain, I look for a way out, but there is none. Then it hit me. There is no pardon in my future, no court of appeals to review my case, or an empathetic friend to hear my story. Nope, my new reality, without Christ, is darkness, the smell of rotten eggs, hunger, thirst, searing heat, gasping for air because of the lack of oxygen, and the painful cries coming from those, like me, who thought it was "cool" to deny Christ.

Looking back, I now realize all that my denials earned me was an eternal trip to the lake of fire, my new forever reality.

IT WOULD HAVE MADE NO DIFFERENCE

Have you ever wondered what your life would have been like without Jesus? I have. While standing in front of Jesus, in my what-if fantasy, I mentioned how I wished I had listened to those who shared the gospel with me. The truth is, it would have made no difference because the Word says, "If anyone's name is not written in the book of life, he (she) was thrown into the lake of fire" (Rev. 20:15).

After reading Revelation 20:15, I praised God for writing my name in His book of life. Because He gave me eternal life, my what-if fantasy will never be my reality. If your name is in His book, it will never be your reality, either. If you are grateful for what He has done for you, why not choose to conduct your life in a manner worthy of His sacrifice (Eph.4:1).

HIS SHEEP REMAIN HIS FOCUS

When I understood why our will has nothing to do with salvation, I wept because God did not have to forgive me and rescue me from Our Lord's wrath, but He did, and like you, I am eternally grateful.

Why did He choose us? Thinking about my past, I often ask myself this question. I know I did not deserve a life with Him. And like you, I am thankful He wrote my name in the Lamb's book. Maybe He will explain why He chose us one day. Until then, we ought to praise the Lord for what He has done because the alternative is unthinkable.

Even as Jesus prepares for the final judgment, His sheep remain His focus. Salvation was God's plan from the beginning, and it will stay this way for eternity. No matter how fair or unfair we might think salvation is, He is the one who holds the key to our eternity in His hands.

18

THE BEMA SEAT JUDGMENT

"The nations were angry, and your wrath has come. The time has come for judging the dead, and for rewarding your servants the prophets and your people who revere your name, both great and small— and for destroying those who destroy the earth."

REVELATION 11:18

While the argument about the timing of the Lord's return for His Bride will continue, at some point, the tribulation will be here, and then we will know for sure. But for now, our differences remain because even if the facts prove otherwise, most teachers will find it difficult to admit they were wrong.

THE PREMILLENNIALISTS' VIEW OF THE BEMA SEAT

While the tribulation takes place, those teachers, who place their faith in a pre-tribulation rapture, share how the Lord will reward His saints, in heaven, for the way we conducted our lives on earth.

Now, you might think this sounds logical based on the billions of believers who are eligible to receive His awards. Even so, we must ask ourselves if it makes sense for Jesus to honor His followers in heaven while He has saints dying for their faith during the Great Tribulation.

Another way to look that this is to ask ourselves, "Will the Lord need seven years to hand out His rewards?"

Revelation 22:12 offers us some insight into this question. How? Jesus said He is returning to this world after the Great Tribulation, and with Him are the rewards He has for His saints, "according to the works they have done." Therefore, it appears the Bema Seat Judgment will take place after He returns, and not before.

Moreover, Revelation 11:18 says, *"The nations were angry, and your wrath has come. The time has come for judging the dead, and for rewarding your servants the prophets and your people who revere your name, both great and small— and for destroying those who destroy the earth."* REVELATION 11:18

In v. 11:18, Jesus places the award's ceremony after the judgment of the saints. He says the time has come for "judging the dead, and for rewarding your servants, the prophets and your people who revere your name, both great and small." In other words, the Award's ceremony, referred to as the Bema Seat Judgment of the saints, does not take place during the tribulation. Instead, it appears to take place after the judgment of the dead or the unredeemed.

If you think about it, why would the Bema Seat take place before Jesus gathers His saints together? Does it make sense to have two award ceremonies, one for those He raptured before the tribulation, and one for those left behind, who supposedly found Christ during the tribulation?

Let's see what the Word has to say about the Bema Seat, where the Lord will judge His saints. But before I do, I would like to share an encounter I once had with the Lord.

GOD GAVE ME A VISION

Driving my car to work one morning, the Lord asked me a simple question. He said, "Lynn, what happens to my people, who continue to sin after they know the truth?" I said, "Lord, I don't know. I guess your grace would cover their sins."

While His question caught me off guard, it did pique my curiosity. On my way home, I decided to examine the scriptures to see if I could find an answer to His question. Although I was not sure what He wanted me to know, I needed to take the time to find out. So, I began my study by turning to Second Corinthians 5:10. It says, "For we must all appear before the judgment seat of Christ, so that each one may receive what is due for what he has done in the body, whether good or evil."

The Bema Seat, according to the Amplified Bible, was "a raised area reached by steps, used as the official seat of a judge." For example, the Olympic games began in Olympia, Greece, during the 3rd and 4th Century BC. Those in charge located their judges near the finish line.[21] This way, they made sure the participants completed the race and received their rewards according to how they finished their event. [22]

In the same manner, Christ will review our "actions, the purpose or motive for doing something, our goals, misuse of His time, the opportunities we seized upon or overlooked, and the ability to do what we were to do." [23]

He told me, "When we stand before Him, we'll feel naked." He qualified His statement by saying, "Grace gets you to heaven, but at the Bema Seat, grace will not cover this judgment." In other words, He is going to hold us accountable for the work we did in His name on earth. Meaning how we spent our time, the work we did in His name, and the way we treated others are all fair game.

Like the Olympics, Jesus will withhold the rewards we might have earned if we fail to conduct ourselves according to His will and purpose for our lives.

How we manage our lives and control ourselves on earth will make a difference in heaven. And, as far as we know, there are no do-overs.

Thus, the rewards we receive, and the responsibilities we have in the next life depends on our words, deeds, and the faithfulness we show toward Him while we remain on earth.

Paul describes our life in Christ in his second letter to the Corinthians by saying, "So whether we are at home or away, we make it our aim to please him. For the love of Christ controls us, because we have concluded this: that one has died for all therefore all have died; and he died for all, that those who live might no longer live for themselves but for him who for their sake died and was raised" (2 Cor. 5:9, 14-15).

The love of Christ should compel us to honor Him in the way we conduct our lives. For instance, the Bible tells us to love others, as He loved us. As for our work, we should do our best to represent Christ by doing good, so that others might see Jesus in us (Matt. 5:16).

GOD'S CALLING ON OUR LIVES

If you compare Peter, John, and the other disciples to the Pharisees, they appear to have nothing to offer because they lacked the upbringing both the Temple Rabbis and the teachers had. Subsequently, I can understand why the Jewish leadership had a difficult time taking Peter and the rest of the disciples seriously.

Knowing this, we should feel encouraged because God does not seek our physical talents to fulfill His kingdom's work. Instead, He uses ordinary people, like us, and births within us the gifts we need to fulfill His calling. The Lord manages this through our prayers, the Holy Spirit's guidance, and His Word.

After all, the Bible says, "Now, when they saw the boldness of Peter and John, and perceived that they were uneducated, common men, they were astonished. And they recognized that they had been with Jesus" (Acts 4:13).

The elder Peter is a fantastic example of courage and faith. Yet, as a younger man, he stumbled along the way, even denied His Lord three times. But despite his many failures, Jesus continued to use him.

Filled with the Spirit and matured in the faith, Peter became the "Rock," the man Jesus used to help guide His people through some terrifying times. Because of his teaching and the courage he displayed, Peter served as an example for other Christians during those difficult times.

For example, many historians believe Emperor Nero had something to do with setting the fire in Rome's slum area. They think Nero used this opportunity to rebuild Rome and install fire codes. But he never admitted it. Instead, he blamed the Christians who resided in Rome. To cover up his possible crime, Nero had them arrested and persecuted.

In blaming the Christians, Nero showed no mercy toward them. He had them imprisoned, tortured, whipped, and crucified. He even lit some up like candles to light his garden at night. Through it all, Peter took his arrest, beatings, and eventually his crucifixion with great courage and without complaint. The fearlessness he displayed inspired others to cope with their fate, in a manner worthy of Christ. [24]

THE LORD EQUIPS THE CALLED

When Peter and John received the Holy Spirit, they obtained the power, the courage, the gifts, and the knowledge often associated with these men. Their insight into the truth, and the spiritual gifts God bestowed upon them, astonished onlookers. After all, the Rabbis' leadership, who were members of the Sanhedrin, considered them to be "uneducated, common men" compared to themselves. But it did not matter. What they said and how they served others caught people's attention, for they knew they had been with Jesus.

To accomplish our work takes faith. Along the way, we will have doubts and fears to overcome. Some of us will feel unworthy to carry out God's calling based on how we conducted our lives before Christ. Others will see what God has in mind for them as impossible tasks because they lack the education or the skill to complete it. But none of these things matter because it's not our work, it's the Lords. And the Lord who calls us to do this work will also equip us to complete the task He called us to do.

"And he gave the apostles, the prophets, the evangelists, the shepherds, and teachers, to equip the saints for the work of ministry, for building up the body of Christ..." EPHESIANS 4:11-12

God will equip you with power, skill, knowledge, finances, people, and the courage necessary to fulfill His calling through you. Yes, in the same manner, He trained Peter and John; the Holy Spirit will do the same for you. And when you finish the task, Jesus will reward you for the faith you displayed, and the love you showed others while carrying out the work He planned for you before the foundation of the world (Eph. 2:10).

THE HALL OF FAITH

"For consider your calling, brothers: not many of you were wise according to worldly standards, not many were powerful, not many were of noble birth. But God chose what is foolish in the world to shame the wise; God chose what is weak in the world to shame the strong; God chose what is low and despised in the world, even things that are not, to bring to nothing things that are, so that no human being might boast in the presence of God." 1 CORINTHIANS 1:26-29

In Hebrews Chapter 11, we read about those faithful men and women who honored God by carrying out their calling. These were ordinary people, just like you and me. And yet, He rewarded their work by placing their names in His "Hall of Faith."

When you think of the great work, Noah, Abraham, Moses, Samson, Jephthah, David, and Samuel did, you might wonder how we could live up to their faith-filled accomplishments.

Besides these men, there were two women whom God recognized for their faith: The first woman is Sarah. God honored her for believing she could conceive long after her childbirth age. And He rewarded her faithfulness with a son named Isaac, the child of the promise. The other is Rahab, the prostitute, who hid the Jewish spies so they could escape their enemies. God rewarded Rahab's faithfulness and courage by placing her son in the line of Christ, for she was the mother of Boaz, the same Boaz who married Ruth. Ruth and Boaz became the parents of Obed, who fathered Jesse, who fathered David.

When we compare the great work of Noah, Moses, David, and others to Sara and Rahab, we could say there is no comparison. But when God saw the faith these two women displayed, He rewarded them by adding their names to His "Hall of Faith." Why? Because they achieved what He called them to do.

By the world's standard, we probably would not have considered Sarah or Rahab for such a reward, but God did because they kept the faith and played an essential role in the life of the Jewish people and the entire world. Thus, His calling has nothing to do with our physical skills, or how significant others might think we are; instead, it's about how great the Lord is, and how He takes ordinary people and equips them to carry out His will. And when the time comes for you to stand before the Bema Seat, He will reward you for the faithfulness you displayed in executing His calling on your life.

Yes, God takes the foolish, the despised, the lowly, the weak, and even the seemingly uneducated, as in John's and Peter's case, to astonish the world. He does this so that we will not take the credit, but give it to Him, the Author, and Finisher of our faith.

God never wants us to boast about our successes because we happen to have the talents and skills necessary to carry out His calling. Instead, the Word says, "Let the one who boasts, boast in the Lord" (1 Cor. 1:31). We give the Lord credit because He became our wisdom from God, along with our "righteousness, sanctification, and redemption" (1 Cor. 1:30). Therefore, whatever we do, we do it unto the Lord, whether ministry-related or in the secular world.

PLANNED BEFORE THE WORLD'S FOUNDATION

"For we are his workmanship, created in Christ Jesus for good works, which God prepared beforehand, that we should walk in them." EPHESIANS 2:10

We discussed how the Lord knew you before the foundation of the world. He also knows the work He has planned for you. Yes, God has a plan for your life's calling, and He will fulfill His purpose through you if you have the faith to carry it out. Also, you must be careful not to disqualify yourself through some sin, doubt, or fear because they can keep you from your destiny. Any of these could prevent you from finishing His calling on your life.

I remember hearing about a woman who seduced her pastor, not for seduction's sake, but to entrap him and then have him removed from the pulpit. So, she recorded the temptation and presented it to the church leadership, who, after reviewing him, fired him. This man left the church in disgrace, and the last I heard, he left the ministry and began working for a new car dealer.

When thinking about the Bema Seat's ties to the early Olympics, my Dad told me a story about his track team and how they forfeited their chance to win the Nebraska High School State Track and Field Tournament.

It was the final event of the meet, and his team was in the lead. All they had to do was win the last relay race, and they would take home the trophy for winning the state tournament.

As the team's coach, Dad never doubted they could win. After all, his runners were the fastest in the state, and winning this relay would seal the deal for his school, Omaha Tech.

In describing the race, Dad shares how the first runner had given them substantial lead, and the second one added to it. But when it came to the third runner, something unexpected happened.

To understand what transpired, you need to know a couple of facts from the past. In those days, runners wore spiked shoes because they ran on cinder tracks. Unlike the asphalt tracks we have today, their spiked shoes provided the athletes the necessary traction they needed to run on cinder without slipping. As for their batons, they were made from bamboo instead of the familiar metal or plastic batons our modern-day relay teams use.

Having these facts in mind, and with the second runner increasing Tech's lead, everything was going as planned. That is until the baton exchange took place between the second and third runners.

For some reason, the baton slipped out of the third runner's hand and landed on the track. In a hurry to retrieve it, the third runner stepped on it and drove his spikes through the baton. Instead of lifting his foot to release it, he tried to pull it free while his body weight and spiked shoes pinned it to the asphalt track.

Well, as you can imagine, his effort shattered the baton into many pieces. Surprised, but not deterred by his misfortune, he carefully grabbed one of the fragments, with his thumb and index finger, and took off.

Now, Let's say you are the fourth runner. You see your third guy way ahead of the competition, so to take home the trophy, all you need is the baton. Well, with your receiving hand behind you and your eyes forward, you wait for the familiar handoff, where the third runner is supposed to slip the baton into your hand. But this time, something felt different.

Instead of receiving the familiar baton, you get a small fragment of what used to be a whole baton. Confused, you look at it, hold it between your thumb and index finger, shrug your shoulders, and take off as if nothing unusual had happened.

At the end of the race, your team is exuberant because the victory earned your school the state title. Ready to receive the team trophy, the stadium announcer says the judges have disqualified Tech's mile relay team because the rules say you must finish the race with the entire baton and not a fragment of it.

Suddenly, your joy disappears, and reality sets in as you realize the disqualification cost your team the state title. Instead of celebrating, your team boards their bus home feeling ashamed and sorrowful for what happened on the track that day.

Just as a track team must run according to the regulations, we are to do the same. Second Timothy 2:5 says, "An athlete is not crowned unless he competes according to the rules."

While Dad's team lost because they broke the rules, Paul warns us about running the race of eternal life. He said, "Do you not know that in a race all the runners run, but only one receives the prize? So, run that you may obtain it" (1 Cor. 9:24).

Paul continues by saying, "Every athlete exercises self-control in all things. They do it to receive a perishable wreath, but we an imperishable" (1 Cor. 9:25).

Likewise, to qualify for the crowns our Lord has waiting for us at the Bema Seat, we must adhere to the rules. If we run according to the rules and do not disqualify ourselves, we win.

Paul also warns us not to run aimlessly but to have a purpose. By doing these, we will not lose our rewards and walk away from the Bema Seat in shame (1 Cor. 9:26-27).

So, be careful not to let doubt and fear overcome you, or some sin overtake you, but run to win, and Jesus will have your reward waiting for you.

THE FIVE CROWNS FOR GOD'S PEOPLE

1. **The Incorruptible Crown:** *Paul was careful not to disqualify himself for this crown by losing his self-control. We receive this crown when we overcome sin by denying our lustful desires through self-control and the power of the Holy Spirit. Yes, the sacrifices we make for God, to carry out His plan and purpose, earns us the incorruptible crown* (1 Cor. 9:26-27).

2. **The Crown of Rejoicing or Rejoicing:** *This crown is the soul winners crown. Believers receive it for leading people to Christ. This reward has to do with our willingness to share the gospel with others* (1 Thes. 2:19-20).

3. **The Crown of Life:** *We win this crown by overcoming the trials we face in life (James 1:12). It's also called the Martyr's Crown. People who suffer for their faith and give up their lives for Christ will receive this crown* (Rev. 2:8-11).

4. **The Crown of Righteousness:** *God's people earn this crown by living a life worthy of Christ's sacrifice.*

Meaning we honor the Lord and look forward to His second coming (2 Tim. 4:8).

5. **The Crown of Glory:** *Pastors and teachers win this crown for faithfully serving the body and teaching them the Word of God as it was written. The Lord holds preachers and teachers accountable for what they teach, and how they hold fast to the truth, in their teaching (1 Pe. 5:1-4).*

CASTING THE CROWNS

"...the twenty-four elders fall down before him who is seated on the throne and worship him who lives forever and ever. They cast their crowns before the throne, saying, 'Worthy are you, our Lord and God, to receive glory and honor and power, for you created all things, and by your will they existed and were created.'"
REVELATION 4:10-11

Once the Lord rewards us with our crowns, we might wonder what is next. Do we wear them? No, the Word says something different. The elders, in vv. 10-11, show us how to honor the Lord with our crowns.

After receiving them, we are to cast our crowns at our Lord's feet, in honor of Him. In addition to the crowns, my guess is there will be other rewards such as our position and the responsibility He gives us in both the Millennial Kingdom and the new heaven and new earth. Therefore, Paul encourages us to strive to earn these crowns.

You may be wondering why Paul concentrated on winning the incorruptible crown. Like you, I wanted to know the reason, so I asked the Lord about it. But since I cannot remember His exact words, I decided to paraphrase what He told me.

He said, "You cannot necessarily know what heaven is like, or what I am like (in a true sense). But you know what it takes to win a medal or a trophy. So, concentrate on them, just as if you were an athlete competing for the Olympics. Learn the rules for each crown, and then strive to win them."

So, why should we run to win a crown? Well, like an Olympic athlete, God wants us to keep our eyes on the prize. This exercise will help us stay focused on what we need to do, along with the changes we need to make in our lives, to earn our reward.

A CHRISTIAN'S TESTIMONY

"I have struggled with an addiction for years. I wanted to rid myself of it, but I could not. Then I decided to try the above. Wanting to win one of the crowns, I chose to keep my eyes on the crown. Since then, like an Olympic athlete, I keep my eyes on the crown. Doing this has helped me stay focused, and I believe it will do the same for you."

APOSTASY AND THE FORFEITING OF OUR REWARDS

The definition of an apostate is one who *defects or disavows their faith*. Most Christians believe these deserters are false believers. Yes, in part, this may be true, but we should not discount Christians who, for one reason or another, walk away from their faith.

Again, I am not sure how prevalent this is, but, as you will see, some of the defections taking place in the book of Hebrews pointed to Christians and not false believers. I must admit I was as surprised as you by this discovery.

I mentioned how God had asked if I knew what happens to believers who continue in sin. His question put me on the path to find out more about the Bema Seat Judgment. My search started with First Corinthians 5:10 and moved on from there.

God then took me to Hebrews Chapter 10, where I learned about the fate of some Christian apostates who left their faith in fear for their lives. Regarding the times, it's my understanding these Jewish believers were abandoning Christ and returning to Judaism to avoid Roman persecution.

Most Bible teachers think these defectors were part of the body of Christ, in the flesh, but not in the Spirit. Meaning, they identified as Christians, but they were not of the faith. So, to save themselves from Roman persecution, they denied their faith and returned to Judaism.

How do we know this? In this part of the letter, the author shows concern about Christians who fall away. We know this because this person "profaned the blood covenant which he was sanctified." The only way one can receive sanctification is through the blood of Christ and the work of the Holy Spirit within us. Now, if this person fails to repent, then it will not go well with him.

It's interesting how the Lord's question matched the first two verses from the passage I read in Hebrews 10. It says, "For if we go on sinning deliberately after receiving the knowledge of the truth, there no longer remains a sacrifice for sins, but a fearful expectation of judgment, and a fury of fire that will consume the adversaries" (Heb. 10:26-27).

Now, please do not get me wrong; I am not talking about the type of sin many Christians face, such as an addiction they might have had before they came to Christ. These are not the acts the author refers to in Hebrews. No, these acts of sin are more sinister.

These saints defiantly ignored Christ and His sacrifice. By upholding desires and beliefs that were contrary to the Word of God, Jesus considered them apostates or people who deserted their Faith. In other words, they turned their backs on Christ and left the church to return to their life under the law.

Why did they walk away? Well, these were Messianic-Jews or former Jews who came to Christ. Because Rome was persecuting the Christians, these saints believed if they returned to Judaism, Rome would spare them. The author of Hebrews warned them about defecting. He said if they failed to repent, they would receive a "fearful expectation of judgment" before the Bema Seat, a.k.a. Christ's judgment reserved for His Saints.

Moreover, the Word says, "For we know him who said, 'Vengeance is mine; I will repay.' And again, 'The Lord will judge his people.' It is a fearful thing to fall into the hands of the living God" (Heb. 10:30-31).

Apostasy is not something true believers want to dabble with, in this life. When times become difficult, instead of considering it and affecting our eternal rewards, it would be better for us to suffer for a little while by enduring our trials with patience and faith rather than lose hope and turn away from the one who gave His life for us. I know this is easy to say because we are not the ones facing Roman persecution.

Likewise, we would have no power to stand firm in such a time without Christ. When persecution comes upon us, the Holy Spirit will give us what we need if we allow Him to work within us to provide us with the faith, the patience, and the endurance we will need to withstand such a trial.

BUILDING ON THE WRONG FOUNDATION

"For no one can lay a foundation other than that which is laid, which is Jesus Christ." 1 CORINTHIANS 3:11

Another way to lose our rewards has to do with building our faith on the wrong foundation, where we fail to form our lives around Christ and God's Word. Instead, we accomplish our work by twisting the interpretation of God's Word to fit our behavior. The result is we find ourselves following a tolerant god we created in our minds to justify our sinful behavior.

One example is the "Health, Wealth, and Prosperity" movement. All through the late '80s and '90s, the purveyors of this movement had people believing God wanted every believer to be healthy, wealthy, and prosperous.

Over the years, unsuspecting believers gave millions of dollars to these false teachers who presented the health, wealth, and prosperity gospel as the truth. In the end, all this gospel did was enrich the false teachers while leaving their adherents, wondering when their big payday would arrive.

The Word addresses the health, wealth, and prosperity-type teaching in 1 Timothy 6:3-5. It says those who teach this have "an unhealthy craving for controversy and for quarrels about words, which produce envy, dissension, slander, evil suspicions, and constant friction among people who are depraved in mind and deprived of the truth, imagining that godliness is a means of gain" (wealth).

There are many ways to build our calling on the wrong foundation. What happens to those who do this? The Word says, "...each one's work will become manifest, for the Day will disclose it, because the fire will reveal it, and the fire will test what sort of work each one has done. If the work that anyone has built on the foundation survives, he will receive a reward." 1 Corinthians 3:13-14

The Lord will test our works. If we build them on the right foundation, we will receive our just reward; Otherwise, the Word says, "If anyone's work is burned up, he will suffer loss, though he himself will be saved, but only as through fire" (1 Cor. 3:15).

Yes, if we build our lives on the wrong foundation, we remain saved, but as someone who has escaped a fire. When I ask my students, "What is the worst thing about a home fire, assuming everyone escapes with their lives?" Their answer always includes losing pictures and family memorabilia.

We see something similar in v. 3:15. The memorabilia, in this case, happens to be our rewards. If we build our faith on the wrong foundation, we will escape the fire. But as for our awards, the inferno will destroy them.

So, make sure you remain faithful to the Lord and build your life on the right foundation because anything less will cost you the rewards the Lord has for you, based on your service to the kingdom, and the faith you displayed throughout your life as a Christian.

19

WHAT ABOUT THESE VERSES

"Do your best to present yourself to God as one approved, a worker who has no need to be ashamed, rightly handling the word of truth."

2 TIMOTHY 2:15

In this chapter, we will look at two verses believers often use to prove free will. We will examine them to see if they show God's intent to save everyone, or if they are using these scriptures out of context. In reviewing the verses, you can see for yourself if they are interpreting these properly or not.

DOES GOD WANT ALL TO COME TO REPENTANCE?

Let's begin by examining Second Peter 3:9. It says, "The Lord is not slow to fulfill his promise as some count slowness, but is patient toward you, not wishing that any should perish, but that all should reach repentance."

Most Christians, who believe in free will, start their defense with this verse. They use it to prove how God desires to save everyone. Is this the case? Are they interpreting this verse correctly?

To understand this verse, we begin our investigation by identifying the author's intended audience. Is it the Lord's elect or the world? The salutation says, "To those who have obtained a faith of equal standing with ours by the righteousness of our God and Savior Jesus Christ" (2 Pe. 1:1).

According to this verse, Peter wrote his letter to those whose faith is on the same level as the apostles. In other words, Peter's intended audience is not the world but the elect.

To help you identify whom the Lord is patient toward, I use the following illustration. Let's say your daughter comes home from a football game. As she walks by, she says, "It was a great game, Mom! Everyone was there." Now, would you interpret this to mean everyone in the world was there? Of course not. As parents, you know her *everyone* points to her friends and not everyone in the world.

Since we know Peter's intended audience is the elect, then who is the *all* as in "all should reach repentance." Well, just as your daughter did not mean the entire world when she said everyone was at the game, Peter never had the whole world in mind either. In his letter, he says God is patient toward you (believers), so "all should reach repentance."

What does patience have to do with this? Whether you believe in free will or predestination, God knows His children, and they are His Son's rightful heirs.

As the Executor of Christ's estate, God will not cut short His offer of redemption by overlooking some of His Son's heirs. Neither will he shorten the time limit. In either case, doing one of these would prevent some of the Lord's heirs from receiving Christ before He returns. An earthly executor would not do this, and neither would our God.

Therefore, we have confidence in God's patience toward us. Because of His patience, the Lord's inheritance remains open until all His heirs, listed in the book of life, receive their gift of salvation. Until then, God withholds His wrath meant for the ungodly.

If you think about it, there is no reason for God to wait for the wicked (those not listed in the Lamb's book of life) to come to the knowledge of Christ because they will never seek after Him. And besides, they are not in His will. For this reason, God will remain patient toward us, until all who are Christ's heirs receive their inheritance.

ALL COME TO THE KNOWLEDGE OF TRUTH

"First of all, then, I urge that supplications, prayers, intercessions, and thanksgivings be made for all people, for kings and all who are in high positions, that we may lead a peaceful and quiet life, godly and dignified in every way. This is good, and it is pleasing in the sight of God our Savior, who desires all people to be saved and to come to the knowledge of the truth." 1 TIMOTHY 2:1-4

In this verse, those who believe in free will defend their position by saying God wants all people to know the truth. But is this the case? Does Paul's letter to Timothy charge him and his flock with the responsibility to tell everyone on the planet about Christ?

Well, vv. 1-4 has nothing to do with sharing the knowledge of Christ with everyone in the world. Instead, they are instructions on how Timothy's flock should pray for the lost.

Paul knew how easy it was to offer supplication, prayer, and intercession for the poor and the oppressed. Regarding God's kingdom, they are the low-hanging fruit. Therefore, instead of wanting everyone to know Christ, the Apostle encourages Timothy and his members to pray for the powerful and those of high standing because God's sheep inhabit all levels of society. Knowing this, Paul writes to Timothy to make sure he does not overlook them (1 Tim. 2:1-2).

Once again, by reading these verses in context, we can see why they have nothing to do with God's desire for everyone to come to the truth.

Paul reminds us to pray for those we refer to as the rich and powerful, for they are the same group Christians often overlook today. Thus, *all people* in verses 1-4, points to a specific demographic rather than everyone in the world.

YOUR PERSPECTIVE WILL SHAPE YOUR VIEW

The key to understanding these verses is to have a proper perspective about God's eternal plan of salvation. If you believe our will has something to do with salvation, then you will see these two examples as representing everyone in the entire world.

However, if you come from the viewpoint where God knows who His people are, then you will understand why He remains patient until He brings all the Lord's heirs into the fold. Also, since the Lord has heirs in all sectors of society, He wants us to pray for the rich and the powerful so that they may know Christ.

Yes, the way we interpret these two verses depends on how we view God's plan of salvation. Again, since the plan of salvation is central to the entire Word of God, how we view it will affect the way we interpret these and other related scriptures in the Bible.

Section V

THE PRACTICAL

"Let your reasonableness be known to everyone. The Lord is at hand."

PHILIPPIANS 4:5

20

MY STRUGGLE WITH GOD'S CALLING

"For the gifts and the calling of God are irrevocable."

Romans 11:29

When I received the gift of salvation in 1985, I could not wait to tell the world about Jesus. I had left my job in Jefferson City, Missouri, and taken a new position in Shreveport, Louisiana. My wife, Mary, and the children had yet to join me, so I called her with the good news. I thought she would be excited about my new faith, but alas, I was not ready for her reaction.

Not knowing what to think about my faith in Christ, she wondered if I was under the Devil's influence before receiving Christ and attending a charismatic church, rather than the denomination we belonged to in Jefferson City, Missouri.

Well, you talk about letting the air out of one's balloon. Coming from a background much different than a charismatic church, and being a new creation in Christ, I did not know how to answer her. Anyway, her reaction was not what I expected.

Looking back, at her reaction, I do not think she understood the need for salvation, nor the excitement I expressed about my being a new creation in Christ Jesus. Of course, I did not have any idea about salvation before receiving Christ, so why would I have expected her to respond any differently.

A few weeks later, Mary joined me in Shreveport. Wanting to find a local church to attend, we decided to visit the one pastored by a neighbor of ours. To this day, it remains one of our favorites because this church conducted its services, including spiritual gifts, in an orderly fashion, according to God's Word.

With my family settled in, I spent time every morning walking and talking with God. In addition to spending time with Him, I attempted to read a new verse each day from a stack of scripture cards I carried with me. To help in my endeavor, I shuffled the cards before taking my walk. By doing this, I hoped to pull a new scripture every day.

Well, it did not work, because after shuffling the cards, I kept pulling the same verse, Psalm 32:8. This verse says, "I will instruct you and teach you in the way you should go; I will counsel you with my eye upon you."

I could not believe how often this verse came up. So, one morning after pulling Psalm 32:8 again, I felt God wanted me to claim this verse as a promise from Him to me, so I did. Being new in the faith, I had no other explanation for it. All I can say is God has kept His promise to teach me in His ways and guide me through my walk with Him.

THE TRAINING BEGINS

Six months after moving to Shreveport, I took a job with a radio network in Jackson, Mississippi. Once we settled in, Mary and I agreed we needed to go church hunting. In talking with my new sales manager, he told me about a startup church called Cornerstone. So, we checked it out, liked it, and decided to attend.

During our time at Cornerstone, I introduced myself to their associate pastor, Dr. Claude Townsend. Hearing how he mentored believers, I asked him if he would consider teaching me. He said he would if I promised to share with others what he taught me. I promised him I would, and he began to teach me from God's Word.

Christian mentoring is a valuable tool for the kingdom. If it had not been for Dr. Townsend, I would not be teaching or writing books and articles based on the Bible today. He was the man God used to instruct me in His ways. In addition to guiding me through the Word, he took the time to teach me how to train others so they could pass onto others what they learned from me.

As I continued to grow spiritually, God drew my wife to Jesus, and she became a believer. I was so happy because we could now move forward together as one in the body of Christ. I cannot tell you what a difference this made in our relationship and our faith. A faith we imparted to our children, hoping they would pass it along to theirs one day, and they have.

GOD COMES CALLING

In 1994, God called me to help set His people free. While seeking Him, He gave me a love for writing. That year, the Lord asked me to write my first book now titled, *Crucified with Him*. After some convincing on His part, I agreed to write it. What I did not know was the impact this book would have on so many lives.

Over the years, our ministry has taught thousands through this book. And thousands of others have received their salvation through our former students' and our partnering pastors' efforts to lead people to Christ. To my joy, God has used this book, and the Holy Spirit's anointing, to help free His people from their addiction and idol worship, just as He promised He would do.

While God has called me to train others and to help believers find their paths to freedom, I came to a place where I began to doubt my salvation. I do not know why, but I knew I did not want to leave this world without Him. All I know is this doubt about my salvation would not go away.

THE DAY GOD CONFIRMED MY SALVATION

I admit I struggled with my salvation over the years. When doubts arose within me, I would say, "God, why did you save me? You know how I conducted my former life before I found you. Why did you do this for me?"

My doubts continued for years until one morning, during prayer, I told God, "I am tired of the shame. I need to know if I am yours or not? If I am, then I'll praise you, Lord. If not, then I will repent and seek you once again. Lord, either way, I need to know."

After praying, I stood up and headed toward the living room, where I kept my Bible." On my way there, I noticed my "Way of the Master Bible" sitting by our microwave. I had just discovered this long-lost Bible a few days before and left it there to keep an eye on it.

Upon seeing it, the Lord stopped me and asked me to pick it up. I said, "Lord, this Bible is the New Testament only; it does not have the Psalms." I then reminded the Lord how He almost always speaks to me through the Psalms. I thought He would agree with me, but He said nothing, so I grabbed the Bible and opened it, hoping the page I turned to would have the answer I needed. But, because this Bible lacked the Psalms, I had my doubts about finding what I needed to hear from God.

Regardless of how I felt, I obeyed Him and read the verses from the middle of the page down. When finished, I said Lord, "I do not see an answer to my question."

Disappointed, yet not surprised because it lacked the Psalms, I was about to close the book when God said, "Lynn, look up!" I raised my eyes and scanned the scriptures toward the top of the page. Only then did I see my answer in bold letters. The Word said, "You are my Son." I could not believe it. Full of joy, I closed the book and praised Him because it's one thing for me to call Him friend; it meant much more to have Him call me friend.

After thanking Him, I said, "God, regarding the word 'Son,' I know this is the big 'S,' and this has to do with Jesus; no matter, I receive it as a small 's' and thank You for confirming my salvation. Lord, telling me this makes all the difference; and so, I will no longer doubt my salvation. Thank you!"

Since then, I stopped questioning my salvation because God confirmed my salvation and erased all my doubts and fears about my standing with Him.

After all, the Creator of the Universe called me His son. What else could He say to convince me? If I continued to wrestle with my salvation, this would make me one of the double-minded people the Word warns us about in James Chapter 1.

Since I did not want to become one of those people, I praised Him then, and I continue to praise Him to this day for what He has done in my life.

A SELF-EXAMINATION OF YOUR FAITH

- Maybe it's time to examine your life. Are you following His commands, or are you living to please the world? Without obedience, we will never have a meaningful relationship with Christ. The only way we can have this type of connection is through our obedience to His commands. If you have failed to obey Him by ignoring or rejecting His truths, please take the time to examine your heart to see if you are of the faith (2 Cor.13:5). Then, seek His forgiveness by confessing your sins and forsaking the rebellious acts this world has to offer.

- We only have one life to get it right. If this is you, why not make today the day you seek Jesus with your whole heart, confess your sins, and choose to follow Him by carrying out His commands. When you do, the Word says He will call you His friend (John 15:14).

- Your obedience will kickstart a beautiful relationship between you and your King. So why wait? If you have not done it already, it's about time you make a place for Him in your heart.

21

A True Believer's Characteristics

"Examine yourselves, to see whether you are in the faith. Test yourselves. Or do you not realize this about yourselves, that Jesus Christ is in you?—unless indeed you fail to meet the test!"

2 Corinthians 13:5

God's Work in a True Believer

- Knowing God's purpose changes our desires. Suddenly, we become interested in attending church, have a hunger for His Word, and want to fellowship with other believers (Phil. 2:13).

- The Holy Spirit quickens us or makes us alive in the Spirit, so we can hear and understand the gospel message of salvation. For instance, before you received Christ, others may have shared the gospel, but the words and the need for Jesus never registered with you. Then, one day, after hearing it again, something clicked where it finally made sense to you. It was then you received Jesus as your Lord and Savior. God's drawing and the quickening of the Holy Spirit make the difference. The Spirit's quickening enabled us to hear and understand the gospel of Christ. You, who were once dead in your trespasses, now have His forgiveness. If you are not familiar with the word "quicken," you will find it in the King

James Version. It means "to make us alive in the Spirit" (1 Pe. 3:18).

- There was a time when our faith was not strong enough to believe in Christ, nor to carry us through the trials we face. Thus, the Lord provided what we needed then, and gives us the faith we need today, as believers, to carry us through the various trials we face. The Word says, "For by the grace given to me I say to everyone among you not to think of himself more highly than he ought to think, but to think with sober judgment, each according to the measure of faith that God has assigned" (Rom. 12:3).

- If we know Jesus is the Christ, who came in the flesh, we are His. Those who deny this truth are of the devil (1 Jn. 4:2-3).

- The Word says if our hearts do not condemn us, then we have confidence before God. As believers, we are aware of our sins. The sinful desires having once given us pleasure, now cause our hearts to condemn us or convict us of sin. When this happens, we are to pray and ask God to forgive us of our sins. When we confess our sins and turn from them, John says we can be confident about God hearing our prayers and answering them (1 Jn. 3:21).

If we are the Lord's, we no longer take pleasure in our sins. Instead, we want to die to them, so we might experience the peace and the joy God had in mind for us through Christ. But you say, I still sin, does this mean I am lost?"

No, if you are struggling to overcome an addictive sin, and you ask the Lord to set you free from the desire, this proves you have Christ. Why? Because the unredeemed rarely feel convicted over their sinful behaviors and thoughts, but you do. And for this reason, you no longer take pleasure in your sins and, instead, you want to overcome them.

Why not cry out to the Lord to remove the desire? And when He does, you are free. The kind of freedom the Lord offers is only available to those who love Christ. Why is this? Because God protects His saints, and "the evil one does not touch him" (1 Jn. 5:18).

- Those who overcome the world have Christ. Our faith conquers the world. When this happens, we will experience victory through Christ and the power of His Holy Spirit (1 Jn. 5:5).

- The Word says when we follow His commands, we are the Lord's friends. How can we know His instructions? We find them in the Bible because He is the living Word of God. Also, God may speak to us through the Holy Spirit. When we hear His voice, we are to do what He asks (John 15:14).

- God will use renewal and transformation to change us from the inside out. When we read God's Word, it changes the way we think, live, act, and speak. These changes take place when we understand and accept His Word as truth. When this happens, the Word renews our minds, transforms our hearts, and changes us from the inside out. As these continue to take place within us, people will notice the difference (Rom. 12:2).

- We are to love one another. When we do, we walk in the light of Christ. On the other hand, if we fail to do this, we walk in darkness. What is this darkness? Imagine standing in the middle of a dark room, trying to find the light switch. You search all around the room, but you cannot find it. It's the same with Christ. Without Him, the light grows dark within us. To turn it on, we must repent and seek Him once more.

While millions, in America, claim Christ, few have had a real salvation experience. To be sure of our salvation, we need to examine ourselves. I added this section to help you explore your life and relationship with God. Paul thought it was vital for us to do this; therefore, we should take it to heart.

LIFEWAY RESEARCH FINDINGS

In a 2016 survey of 3,000 believers conducted by Lifeway Research found the following:

- A significant number of those who call themselves believers "embrace ancient errors condemned by all major traditions." [25]

- 70% believe in the doctrine of the Trinity, while 60% believe Jesus is both human and divine. The same survey found over 50% believe Jesus "to be the first and greatest being created by God." [26]

- 70% of those surveyed believe in the one true God. Another 64% believe God honors all religions, including the polytheistic religions. [27]

- The evangelicals or those whom the survey described as the most devoted followers did not fare much better. 70% thought Jesus was a created being. 56% said the Holy Spirit is a divine force, but not a person. And 28%, up from 9% in a previous survey, agreed the Holy Spirit is not equal to the Father and the Son. [28]

"What did those involved with the research think about their findings? "The results of this survey ought to embarrass all of us. But they should also serve as a kick in the pants to re-familiarize ourselves with our religion—or at least our history. There is no excuse to be a nation of heretics. But even that is preferable to being a nation of ignoramuses." [29]

How can we defend the faith and pass along the truth if we do not know it? As a Christian, I have wondered why some of the more popular doctrines are not from the Bible. Yet, many of God's people defend them, believing they are from God's Word.

As saints, we must shore up our beliefs to make sure we are teaching the truth and not what people think is the truth or what is popular or politically correct. We owe this to ourselves, others, and our Lord.

GOD EXPECTS US TO SEEK HOLINESS

The Word says God never changes (Mal. 3:6). It also reminds us He is holy; therefore, we are to be like Him (1 Pe. 1:16).

Israel and Judah discovered what happens to nations when people believe God accepts their sinful behavior. While God loved them, He never let Israel or Judah get away with their rebellious acts against Him, and He will not overlook our sins either.

Our walk, how we live, and how we serve the Lord, speak volumes about our faith. If we love the Lord, we will honor His Word. If not, we will ignore His Word or twist it to fit our beliefs, forsake the fellowship we have with other believers, and run with the world. Yes, we will become like those who praise the Lord with their mouths but never offer their hearts to Him.

THE STATE OF BELIEVERS

"Not everyone who says to me, 'Lord, Lord,' will enter the kingdom of heaven, but the one who does the will of my Father who is in heaven." MATTHEW 7:21

Jesus speaks of those who appear to do great things for Him but fail to carry out His will. When He said only those "who do the will of the Father" ENTER the kingdom, He is not speaking about their need to carry out His ultimate will for their lives as many believe.

Instead, their failure to carry out *His will* speaks to their lost state because they had not *entered the kingdom.* John 6:40 says, "For this is the will of my Father, that everyone who looks on the Son and believes in him should have eternal life, and I will raise him up on the last day."

So, while the men in Matthew 7:21 did great things, they were false teachers because they never entered the kingdom of God by fulfilling God's will to receive Christ as their Lord and Savior.

It's easy to claim Christ; it's more challenging to have Him. Only those whom the Father draws to Jesus will hear the good news and receive Him as their Lord and Savior. In doing so, they carry out His will and enter the new heaven and new earth.

22

SHARING THE GOSPEL

"Go therefore and make disciples of all nations, baptizing them in the name of the Father and of the Son and of the Holy Spirit."

MATTHEW 28:19

When reading the book of Acts, I do not recall the apostles sharing the gospel by telling the lost how GOD LOVES THEM. Do you? Instead, when speaking to the Gentiles, they shared how the real God was not among the idols the Gentiles worshiped. And in the case of the Jews, the apostles explained why they were responsible for our Savior's death. For this reason, they needed to repent and receive Him as their Lord and Savior.

Knowing God's plan of salvation begins with predestation benefits us. Why? First, it's the truth. And the truth is what we are to seek.

Next, knowing His plan gives us the confidence we need when sharing the gospel with others. If those we witness to are His, then God will draw them to Christ; if they are not His, He will not usher them to you. Also, since we are incapable of saving anyone, all we can do is share the gospel and let God increase the kingdom. He does this by giving His sheep a measure of faith so they might believe (Rom. 12:3).

May I ask you this question? When you meet unbelievers, can you tell which of them are God's elect? I am guessing your answer is, *"NO!" IF THIS IS THE CASE,* then why be so concerned about it? All the Lord asks us to do is share the gospel and let Him give the increase (1 Cor. 3:7).

Imagine you are a new salesperson in a corporation where the top seller volunteers to help you close your deals until you feel comfortable with their system. Do you think it would help you get your sales off the ground quicker?

What God does for us is better than this. When God guides a potential believer to us, it's like having all the best salespeople who ever lived helping you secure your deals. Still, this would not come close to what God and the Holy Spirit do for you and the one you share the Gospel with and lead to Christ.

You see, you are the one who delivers the message to the unbelieving souls, while God and His Holy Spirit arrange the divine appointment, make it so the prospect can understand the gospel, and then they close the deal for you by working on the person's heart and mind. Therefore, instead of fighting predestination, you need to know those whom God listed in the book of life are your best, prequalified prospects. You may not know them, but God does, and He will guide them to you. All you need to do is ask Him to send them and watch what He does. After all, God looks for believers who want to go and share the good news with His sheep in waiting.

Being in sales for almost five decades, I found it much easier to close a prequalified referral than it was to find a new prospect who knew nothing about the company or the service we offered. Likewise, God will send you His prequalified candidates. All you need to do is keep your eyes and ears open to the opportunities to share the gospel with them.

DOES PREDETERMINATION LIMIT GOD?

Many, who have trouble with the doctrine of election, believe it limits God and their efforts to share the gospel. I mentioned how, when I talk to believers about this doctrine, the word "limit" often comes up. In their minds, they believe this doctrine restricts their outreach efforts. These people also feel those who believe in predetermination never concern themselves with sharing the gospel. Instead, they think those who credit predetermination, make little effort to reach the lost and wait for God to do it. Consequently, some refer to those who believe God chooses as "the frozen chosen."

Recently, I met a couple who attended a church where predestination is central to their doctrine. In talking with them, they mentioned how their church supports 300 missionaries around the world. Now, I imagine this number, supported by one church, will outpace most churches in the U.S. I heard nothing that caused me to think their doctrine hindered their missionary work or kept them from participating in their outreach efforts.

For those who believe predetermination limits our efforts to share the gospel, may I ask you this question, "Were the apostles negatively affected by their belief in the doctrine of election?"

I do not recall hearing them complaining *about this matter to God or anyone* else, do you? Think about it. They referred to themselves as the elect of God. Meaning, God chose them for salvation. If it never limited the apostles' ability to share the gospel and reach people for Christ, why should it deter us?

To show you what I mean, Paul wrote the following to the Thessalonians. He said, "But we ought always to give thanks to God for you, brothers beloved by the Lord, because God chose you as the firstfruits (from the beginning) to be saved, through sanctification by the Spirit and belief in the truth." 2 Thessalonians 2:13

Instead of limiting our efforts to share the gospel, His predetermination should excite us to realize we are not in charge of eternity. God, the Holy Spirit, and Jesus Christ have this responsibility. As for our involvement, we are only the messengers.

To this day, when God provides the opportunity by drawing other believers to me, I look forward to teaching them about our faith and what it means to live a life worthy of His sacrifice. So, why not share the gospel knowing God is in charge? You see, it's not about you having to save people; instead, it's about the Father drawing them to Jesus and using you to share the gospel so they can learn about the inheritance awaiting them in Christ.

EPILOGUE

"For his invisible attributes, namely, his eternal power and divine nature, have been clearly perceived, ever since the creation of the world, in the things that have been made. So they are without excuse."

ROMANS 1:20

As you might have noticed, I relied on a limited number of outside sources to present the doctrine of election or predestination in this book. Why? Because I wanted to show you what the Bible says about our inheritance in Christ. I chose not to use Calvin, Pink, McArthur, or some other Reformer to persuade you because I wanted the Bible to stand on its own.

This book was fourteen years in the making. The final piece came to me through a recorded sermon. The teacher was not using the scriptures, in the video, to prove the doctrine of election. No, He read them as part of an entire passage to support his sermon about what the new heaven and earth will be like for the Lord's people. When I heard the scriptures, I knew God gave them to me. I needed them to complete the picture of His logical plan of salvation.

While writing this book, I came across an article dealing with the doctrine of election. The pastor who wrote it began by claiming *predestination is of the devil*.

After reading the article, I felt the need to reach out to him. It was not my intention to argue with him but to caution him about his attribution. The rabbis in the Old Testament did the same when they attributed the of the work of the Holy Spirit to Satan. In Matthew 12:31-32, the Word warns us not to do this. Anyway, his website's contact form was down, and I moved on.

God's logical plan of salvation never changes. It's not our plan; it's His. Hence, we are to be like Abraham, where we receive the good news about our inheritance, in Christ, with joy and gladness.

JESUS IN THE GARDEN

"Father, if you are willing, remove this cup from me. Nevertheless, not my will, but yours, be done." Luke 22:42

I admit, I thought I was through with this manuscript when the following illustration came to mind. As it unfolded, I knew I had to use it in this book.

You see, Jesus was in the garden, praying to His Father, and He began to sweat blood. The medical term for this is Hermatidrosis. It happens when someone is under *extreme anguish*.[26] The Lord then asked if there was any other way, and the angels strengthened. Him. He answered by saying, "Not my will by yours be done."

Why this verse? Knowing whose will it is begins with the one who initiates the action. In this case, God's will was for Jesus to die on the cross. As for Jesus, He understandably wanted to know if there was another way. No doubt, He knew what He was about to face.

Agreeing with His Father and carrying out His plan was not an act of His will, but His Father's will. Jesus understood this when He assured His Father by saying, "Not my will, but yours be done."

Likewise, the Father initiated the call on your life when He, through the Holy Spirit, drew you to Jesus. After all, it was His will for you to have eternal life.

By saying, "No!" to Jesus, you would have exercised your will. However, when you agreed to receive Christ as your Lord and Savior, you carried out the Lord's will for your life, and not yours. After all, yours would have been the way of the world, while God's will is for you to spend eternity with Him.

So, this illustration clarifies whose will was in play. Jesus said, "Not my will, but yours be done." He never said, "Okay, Father, I will say 'Yes!' to your plan for me," making us think His affirmation would have been an exercise of His will. No, Jesus knew the difference. Jesus assured His Father that He would carry out God's will rather than find another way.

Therefore, when the Father draws us to Jesus, He initiates the action. And when we receive His inheritance by affirming our faith in Christ, we carry out His will. Thus, the only way to exercise our intention, in this matter, would be to refuse His offer.

But as the Word says, when the Father is in the mix, all we can do is receive His offer (John 6:37). And in doing so, we carry out His will for our life and not ours. Thus, when the Father interrupts our plans, we experience a "Not my will, but yours be done" moment, just as Jesus did.

Thank you for reading this book. I pray it opened your eyes to God's plan of salvation and the inheritance He has waiting for those who are His.

In telling my story, I intended to share my struggles with you because you need to know, if you are struggling with your salvation, you are not alone.

It was not easy for me to let go of the idea that God loves everyone. But I must be honest with you, learning about predetermination changed how I view the Bible, and it led me to seek and understand His deeper truths because His plan is central to the entire Word of God.

If you still have some doubts, may I suggest you take time to seek the Lord and review some of the verses included in this book by reading them in context within the chapter or passages surrounding them?

I wish you well in your walk with the Lord. I pray it will encourage you to continue to build your life upon the right foundation by standing firm in the faith and keeping your eyes on Christ and the crowns He has waiting for you.

NOTES

1 *Americans Draw Theological Beliefs from Diverse Points of View,* Barna Group, https://www.barna.com/research/americans-draw-theological-beliefs-from-diverse-points-of-view/

2 *The Five Points of Calvinism and Arminianism,* https://www.fivesolas.com/cal_arm.htm

3 *Who was Charles Finney,* Got Questions.org, https://www.gotquestions.org/Charles-Finney.html

4 ibid

5a Phillip R. Johnson, *A Wolf in Sheep's Clothing,* http://www.romans45.org/articles/finney.htm, Copyright, 1998,1999, All Rights Reserved.

5b ibid

6 *Augustine quote,* https://www.shmoop.com/quotes/love-the-sinner-hate-the-sin.html

7 *Mahatma Gandhi Quote*; AZQUOTES, https://www.azquotes.com/quote/354905

8 *The Beit-Midrash,* https://www.jtsa.edu/the-rabbinical-school

9 Timothy Willimas and Elizabeth Diaz, *United Methodists Tighten Ban on Same-Sex Marriage and Gay Clergy,* New York Times, https://www.nytimes.com/2019/02/26/us/united-methodists-vote.html

10a Amanda Marcotte, <u>Religious Leaders who gave up Their Faith and Became Outspoken Atheists and Agnostics</u>, Alter Net, March 26, 2013, https://www.alternet.org/2013/03/5-religious-leaders-who-gave-faith-and-became-outspoken-atheists-and-agnostics/

10b ibid

11 Jeffrey Jones, <u>US Church Membership Down Sharply in Past Two Decades</u>, Gallup, April 2019. https://news.gallup.com/poll/248837/church-membership-down-sharply-past-two-decades.aspx

12 Jonathan Merritt, <u>Americas Epidemic of Empty Churches</u>, Nov 2018, The Atlantic, https://www.theatlantic.com/ideas/archive/2018/11/what-should-america-do-its-empty-church-buildings/576592/

13 Rise of Satanism in America, Daily Mail May 2020, https://www.dailymail.co.uk/news/article-6616577/The-rise-Satanism-America-members-dont-ACTUALLY-worship-devil-push-activism.html

14 Leonard Blair, <u>Mega-Church Pastor Slams Christianity and Quits</u>, Leonard Blair, Christian Post, May 2019, https://www.christianpost.com/news/after-40-years-megachurch-pastor-slams-christianity-and-quits-deacon-claims-he-had-affair.html

15 *Denarius,* Bible Study Tools,

https://www.biblestudytools.com/dictionary/denarius/

16 *Jews in the End Time Prophecies*, Lion and the Lamb Ministries, https://christinprophecy.org/articles/the-jews-in-end-time-bible-prophecy/

17 *David and the Millennium,* https://bibletrack.org

18 ibid

19 *Sulfur*, https://en.wikipedia.org/wiki/Sulfur

20 https://www.pbs.org/wgbh/frontline/article/what-does-solitary-confinement-do-to-your-mind/

21 https://en.wikipedia.org/wiki/Olympic_Games

22 *What is the Bema Seat,* Josh Toupos, Amos 37.org, https://amos37.com/the-bema-seat/

23 ibid

24 *Nero's Rome Burns*, The History Channel, https://www.history.com/this-day-in-history/neros-rome-burns

25-29*Survey Finds Most American Christians are Actually Heretics,* The Fedralist.com, https://thefederalist.com/2016/10/10/survey-finds-american-christians-actually-heretics/

26 *Why did Jesus Sweat blood in the Garden,* Got Questions, https://www.gotquestions.org/sweat-blood-Jesus.html

ABOUT THE AUTHOR

Lynn is an author and radio co-host of GodFire Radio. He serves as President of GodFire RDO, a ministry dedicated to training teachers, helping addicts find their paths to freedom, and growing the mission field through their international CALL Schools.

What do people say about Lynn's writing? *He can take the most difficult truths in the Bible and make them easy to understand.*

After spending fourteen years putting all the pieces together, Lynn will tell you it shocked him to see how much of what we have been told about God's plan, including the book of Revelation, is not in God's Word. Discover God's entire plan of salvation from Genesis to Exodus as Lynn Sheldon takes you through the Word and shows you how God's plan never wavers.

Crucified with Him: Knowing Who You Are in Christ. It's an excellent Disciple training book, teaching you, you work with God in chronological order. This book includes a Leader and Student Guide. Perfect for mentoring, youth studies, adult studies, and small group studies. Also available in Hispanic.

Send us your order link, and we will send you a free Leader's Manual for a more in-depth study background to help you with the Leader's guide in the book.

No More Namby Pamby: Courageous Christianity for young men, ages 17 to 34.

Teach with a Purpose: Have a desire to train others in the faith, this book will help you become a great Bible teacher.

Chasing God's Will: You want to know how to spot God's will for your life? Did you know His will has different stages? This book will teach you about each stage, in your Christian walk, and show you the characteristics of each.

Birthmark: Did you know God marks His people with a Birthmark. Find out what it is and how it separates God's people from the wicked who will never receive Christ.

Ambassadors: You are one of Christ's Ambassadors to His Kingdom. Meaning you have a governmental responsibility to carry out God's plan.

Battle Plans: Do you work with addicts, or struggling with other sins in your life? This workbook is an excellent self-study for you to have. It will teach you how to become victorious through spiritual warfare.

Once you finish this book, we suggest you read "Returning to Holiness," by Dr. Gregory Frizzell. Please make sure you read it in a meditative, prayer, manner. "Battle Plans" prepares you for war, and "Returning to Holiness" places you on the battlefield.

MAKE NOTES

Made in the USA
Monee, IL
25 August 2020

38159765R00105